FROM THE GARDEN TO

THE GLASS HOUSE

An Undiplomatic Look at the

United Nations

Abdelkader K Abbadi

FROM the GARDEN TO THE GLASS HOUSE

An Undiplomatic Look at the United Nations.

Published by CreateSpace, an Amazon company.

ISBN: 1517500303
ISBN 13: 9781517500306

To my wife, children, grandchildren, and all those who strive to make our world more peaceful.

Foreword

I thank my old friend Dr. Abdelkader Abbadi for inviting me to write the foreword to his book. I have enjoyed reading the manuscript very much. I would like to make three comments in my foreword.

Dr. Abbadi's life journey has been a miraculous one. He was born to loving but humble parents in a small village, Zaouia-Cheikh, of one thousand people, near the Atlas Mountains. His maternal grandparents actually lived in a cave. Dr. Abbadi's family home had no running water, electricity, toilets, beds, or kitchen equipment.

When Dr. Abbadi was five years old, the French colonial official announced that all children in the village had to enroll for school. Dr. Abbadi proved to be a good student. He completed his middle school in Azrou, a village 150 kilometers from home. From Azrou, Dr. Abbadi went on to the capital, Rabat, to complete his baccalaureate at the famous Lycée Moulay Youssef in 1957.

In 1958, Dr. Abbadi was awarded a Fulbright Fellowship to study in the United States. This was a life-changing opportunity. Dr. Abbadi went first to Lawrence, Kansas, to study English. He then studied at the

Fresno State College in Fresno, California. After a year, he succeeded in getting a transfer to the University of California at Berkeley, and the rest, as they say, is history.

Second, after completing his PhD in political science at Berkeley, Dr. Abbadi joined the United Nations (UN) Secretariat in 1967. After thirty years of distinguished service, he retired in 1997. His last post was that of the director of the African division, in the Department of Political and Security Council Affairs. During my thirteen years as Singapore's permanent representative to the UN (in New York), I had many opportunities to work with Dr. Abbadi and to observe him in carrying out his responsibilities. I had formed a favorable impression of him. I found him to be extremely intelligent and well informed. He always carried out his responsibilities competently and impartially. I found him to be a man of integrity and a perfect gentleman. He treated everyone with courtesy and kindness.

Third, the book contains Dr. Abbadi's thoughts and reflections on, and suggestions about, the UN and the future. Dr. Abbadi is very frank in his appraisals of the various secretaries-general he worked under. He has many valuable thoughts about what ails the UN and suggestions about the reforms that are needed. He loves the UN and is a firm believer in its ideals as enshrined in the UN Charter. In view of this, I was very disturbed to read that the idealism of his generation of UN officials has been replaced by cynicism. I was also disturbed to read that, over the years, the process of recruitment, appointment, and promotion has been increasingly politicized. It seems that the meritocratic system has been increasingly compromised. This is bad news. I hope that all those who love the UN and believe in its ideals will treat this as a clarion call to take action. We live in an increasingly interconnected and interdependent world. We need more, not less, global governance. The UN system plays an indispensable role in global governance.

Professor Tommy Koh

Ambassador-at-Large, Ministry of Foreign Affairs

Singapore

Preface and Acknowledgments
The Long Journey

From the cave where I lived with my grandparents in my native village in the Middle Atlas Mountains, Morocco, to the global society that shaped my personality as a global citizen, this is a road less often traveled and a very long one. It has been a road of growth, discoveries, excitement, and passion. This is the path that took me away from the security of my local village to the immensity of a new and much wider world, fraught with uncertainties but blessed with unexpected promises. Thrown in isolation in a small town in the US Midwest, I discovered American societal values of simplicity, practicality, and openness. I later found myself in the vast and turbulent community of the Bay area in California in the sixties, where I acquired both confidence and knowledge and began to prepare to embark on a road much wider and more complex than the one I had known in my earlier years. In the course of this journey, I unexpectedly met celebrities, experienced exciting true stories in my path of learning as we shall see, traveled on diplomatic missions, and fulfilled with passion my professional duties at the United Nations. The end of this extraordinary journey is the rediscovery of its own beginnings—that is, communion with nature, embracing the spiritual dimension of life, and once again enjoying the blessings of the simple life.

My thanks go to Regina Dizon, Reynaldo Naval and Ryan Osswald for their technical assistance, to my wife for her patience and constant encouragement, and to Desirée Snyder for proofreading this manuscript.

Introduction
My Morocco

When I was a boy in Morocco, we learned in detail how many tons of potatoes were raised in the various provinces of France, but our teachers did not familiarize us with the great American values: the inalienable rights to life, liberty, and the pursuit of happiness. Today Moroccan children learn in school that Morocco was the first country to sign a treaty with America—back in 1777! The two countries share many values of tolerance, stability, and education. The friendship is still strong. Today Morocco is a constitutional monarchy, somewhat like Great Britain, with a growing economy and a flourishing democracy.

I was born in a tiny village in North Africa, in the Atlas Mountains, somewhere in the cold season, perhaps in 1937. As we will see later, there were no birth records in the village. Franklin D. Roosevelt was in the White House, and World War II was brewing around us. I knew little of life outside my village, even though Europe was only eight miles away. I lived at the foot of the Atlas Mountains and began to love the forests. Mountains stand in the northern Rif region, in the middle where we lived, and in the south where the Sahara desert begins. With its high sand dunes and desert pavement of black rock, it is breathtakingly beautiful. During World War II, Winston Churchill loved to look at it out of the window of his suite at the famous Mamounia Hotel in Marrakech. Today the hotel is a tourist attraction. Churchill painted the scenery during his summer vacation. Because it is a land of sunshine and snow, of fertile plains and arid deserts, Morocco has sometimes been described as the "French California."

Why French? Morocco was occupied by France from 1912 to 1956, under the so-called Protectorate Treaty. French troops initially invaded the coastal areas, supposedly to restore stability among the warring tribal factions. In fact, France had a different aim: to appropriate Morocco's natural resources and vast farms. The French occupation and colonization progressed from the coastal shores to the mountain ranges and was not completed until 1932. The French built railroads, highways, bridges, water treatment plants, and hospitals. What affected me was the educational system they introduced in order to communicate with Moroccan citizens.

In school, I learned more French than Arabic. Arabic, which many of us spoke at home, was taught as a foreign language, and for only one hour per week. I wanted to speak good Arabic, so I studied on my own, by candlelight, under the covers, when the school supervisor had gone to bed. Moroccan girls did not attend school in those days. There was a single girl in my high school class. Her father was French and was the director of the school. The school housed about two hundred boys from various villages of the region. During my boyhood, the French influence was very strong, despite sporadic fights to regain independence. While in high school, I participated in the fight for independence, in a peaceful way, by encouraging, in writing, the Moroccan collaborators with the French authorities to cease that collaboration. This episode I relate in my book *Le Maroc Indépendant* (2013).

On January 11, 1944, the main political party in the country, Istiqlal, issued a declaration asking the French authorities to grant independence. The French response was to imprison or exile all the party's leaders. During World War II, world leaders met in Casablanca, where they agreed on "unconditional surrender" of the Axis forces. The American president Franklin D. Roosevelt also privately met with King Mohammed V and assured him that the United States supported Morocco's wish to win independence from France.

Mohammed V successfully negotiated with France for the independence of Morocco, and in 1957, when I was twenty, took the title of king. His successors, of the Alaouite dynasty, still rule the country. Since Morocco recovered its independence, the country and the United States continue to strengthen their ties. The American Legation in Tangier—the first consulate established by America in 1787—is still standing as a historical monument on the Rue D'Amérique, a celebration of Moroccan-American friendship.

On August 20, 1953, the French arrested Sultan Mohammed Ben Youssef on orders from Paris. The sultan had refused to abdicate the throne when the French requested it. They burst into the king's bedroom in the Royal Palace, seized him while he was still in his pajamas, and flew him and his family to Madagascar. They then installed Mohamed Arafat, an unknown figure, as the new king of Morocco. Despite the fact that Sultan Mohammed Ben Youssef was three thousand miles away, the nationalists took up his quest for Moroccan independence.

All the political parties called on their members to engage in demonstrations and strikes. The Army of Liberation was formed to fight French occupiers in the northern mountains, the central Atlas, my birth area, and the southern desert. I witnessed the activities of the political parties. They distributed literature at night, calling on the Moroccans to engage in activities to gain independence. More than ever before, people saw in Sultan Mohammed Ben Youssef the symbol of liberation, a hero who had sacrificed his throne and the interests of his family for the sake of his country. He became so popular that Moroccans would stand on their roofs to see the king's image on the moon. This vision was reported by the press, and people all over the country believed it.

His popularity, in turn, contributed to the momentum of the fight for independence. The nationalist parties and the Army of Liberation intensified their fight. Despite the incarceration of major leaders, the exile of some leading families, and the torture practiced by the French authorities, Moroccans fought harder and harder for their independence. They were encouraged by Franklin D. Roosevelt's promise to endorse the country's recovery of its sovereignty.

Then the French government, in a complete reversal of their decision to exile the monarch, decided to bring him back in full honor. Thus they began negotiations toward Morocco's independence. When Sultan Mohammed Ben Youssef returned to Rabat, the capital, on

November 18, 1955, he was greeted as a hero by thousands of citizens assembled in front of the Royal Palace. A few months after, the independence agreement with France was signed on March 2, 1956.

Since then, Morocco has been trying to establish democratic institutions and to develop its own economy. The sultan's title was changed to King Mohammed V. A new government was formed, and a national army was created. The move toward democracy was slow. The first few years were marred by a sluggish economy and social unrest. I was a student in Rabat at that time, and could see that Morocco's embrace of democracy was going to take more time. A progressive government was established just before I went to America, but it did not last too long. It was abruptly ended in 1960. From 1960 to 1998, Morocco witnessed a period of repression, exile, and disappearance of party leaders. There was no national consensus, and the country was marked by fragmentation. Fifty years after these disheartening events, I published a history of Morocco's struggle—ultimately a successful one—to operate as a true democracy. It was not until 1998 that the country came to know a period of détente. By this time, King Hassan II, son of King Mohammed V, called on the leaders of the main opposition party to form a new government and tried to foster political, economic, and social reforms, with mixed results.

Today, Morocco is moving toward a new phase, characterized by more freedoms, more rights (including those of women) and by a remarkable state of security and stability. More investments are coming into the country. Several world leaders and heads of institutions have recently lauded the moderation and stability of Morocco, including President Barack Obama.

Some, myself included, see the country as a model for others. Indeed, in the midst of the current agitation and turmoil of the nations that have undergone the Arab Spring and have been affected by the spread of terrorism, Morocco can be viewed as an island of stability. It is reinforcing the values of freedom and human rights, and is progressively balancing the powers of the executive, the legislative, and the judiciary. For example, it has, in November 2014, decided to do away with the institution of torture. It is now considering the abolition of capital punishment.

Chapter 1
Born Free in the Gardens

The Ouabidalla Mountains stand high, as a part of the Middle Atlas Mountains in Morocco. In the winter, the summit is covered with snow, above the dry land, like Arizona. At the base of the Ouabidalla Mountains, life swarms in all its aspects, nurtured by the clean, brilliant spring that emerges from under a large rock. A narrow stream crosses the village, showing its movements over clear and tiny stones polished over the years. Members of the Ouabidalla tribe come to fill out their pitchers daily with the cold water of the spring, and life in the hamlet centers on this little stream. The stream pursues its course, meandering around rocks. It spreads some distance away from the village, as it is divided among the vegetable and cereal plots of the small farmers in the area. In the spring and summer, these fields provide the tomatoes, onions, peppers, corn, and cereals that the members of the local community take to another village down the slope and exchange for tea, sugar, spices, shoes, and clothes.

These Moroccans are Berbers, the country's predominant ethnic group; they are tall, traditionally dressed, with white turbans around their heads. They raise cattle, sheep, and goats. Just below the spring, a mud house borders the clear and sparkling stream. The house still stands tall today, simple and devoid of any modern amenities. The door of the house faces the creek, and in front of its opposite side stand majestically two old walnut trees, which would over the years attract me as a child by providing an abundance of nuts. The inhabitants were actually my relatives from my grandmother's side. They were three brothers: M'hamed, Mohamed and Hussein, together with a sister, Aabicha, who passed away in 2014.

Down the slope, three or four miles away, appears the village of Zaouia-Cheikh, the corner where I was born. When? Well, my guess is sometime during a winter, in the year...who knows? My family did not keep calendars and written records, so when I needed a birth certificate for my passport as a teenager, my parents made up one from memory. They estimated that I was born at the beginning of the year 1937, but this reckoning meant nothing to them.

The author before his native house being repaired, in 2013.

In my time, Zaouia-Cheikh was a poor, small village of perhaps a thousand people, mainly shopkeepers and farmers, or should I say, gardeners? Life in the village, as in Ouabidalla, was centered on a river, three meters wide, originating about three miles up at the base of the hill. As in Ouabidalla, the river was crystal clear, dividing itself into several branches to irrigate small fields, orchards, and olive groves. Everyone shared in the bounty of the river: mules, horses, donkeys, women, and children. Frogs and turtles took their sunbaths on stones protruding from the river. Life was simple: no industry, electricity, telephones, cars, sanitation, or health facilities. People walked in the fields, managed tiny shops, harvested crops, or rested in the shade of the olive trees in the market place and hills and borders of the village. The inhabitants lived the life of antiquity.

I was born in a small, two-room house, located in the old center of Zaouia-Cheikh, in a district called Zaouia Laqdima. The house had no amenities such as kitchen equipment, beds, electricity, running water, or bathrooms. Instead of the latter, there was a hole in the ground in the small court, which was about four meters wide by ten meters long. I lived with my parents, grandparents, and two relatives, a total of seven persons in a two-bedroom mud house, in a neighborhood of seven similar houses, attached one to the other. The doors were always open; the parents knew each other and the children, too. There was no privacy.

As children, we ate lunch in one house and dinner in the next. It did not matter. The neighbors were like one big family. The houses formed a rectangle around a court, with a big wooden door leading out to the street. Above the door, on the upper side of the wall, there was a big nest of storks, feeding their babies, or raising their pink beaks and making strange noises as if they were praying. In front of the door, there was a field full of cactus plants, alongside fig and pomegranate trees.

A few meters down the slope, a creek, which formed from the Tamda River, bordered a series of small mud houses before it spread its water, irrigating the old olive trees. It finally joined another river that was half-dry in midsummer. Further down, at the edge of the olive trees, another tributary of Tamda fed the three old stone mills dating from the Roman Empire. Down the slope began a series of small orchards, wheat and cornfields, and vegetable gardens. Finally, in the distant horizon, the river Um Rabii, which originates in Khenifra, about fifty miles to the north of Zaouia-Cheikh, ran. Um Rabii is the longest river in Morocco. It crosses several regions, meandering, before it consumes itself by joining the Atlantic Ocean, at the point of the coastal city of Azemour.

Along the elevated left bank of the Tamda River, there were a number

of caves formed as a result of digging the dirt that built the mud houses

in Zaouia-Cheikh. My maternal grandparents lived in one of these caves.

When my mother visited her parents, she took me with her, and we

sometimes spent the night in the cave. I was four years old. There was no

lighting, only a candle. A hole in the ground of the cave, surrounded by

small stones, served as a stove. The soup cooked in a clay pot, over the

small pieces of firewood my grandmother collected from the forest. We

slept on blankets, directly on the floor. But strangely, the cave was not

cold in the winter, as it had only a small entrance. It was cool and

comfortable during the summer days. I still remember the days and

nights I stayed in the cave. After the village began to develop in the

forties, most of the caves disappeared.

I spent my early years in this village wandering with my four or

five friends among the narrow streets and vegetable and olive fields,

playing below old olive trees, and swimming or fishing in the Tamda or

Um Rabii Rivers. One day we found ourselves in the vegetable field that

belonged to one of my uncles. There were plenty of melons and mouth-

watering cucumbers growing over the grass. We asked my uncle to give us a few watermelons. He said that they were not yet ripe, but in due course, he would be happy to let us have some to take home. Like all youngsters, we did not have the patience to wait until the sweet red fruits were ready for consumption. We therefore resolved to come back to the garden and help ourselves.

One warm afternoon in the following week, we met at the outskirts of the village and started our journey toward the tempting garden, about three miles down the slope, and a mile away from Um Rabii. And, just as each of us bent down and began to detach the green melons that showed a mosaic design on their skin, suddenly my uncle stopped the mule he was riding, a few steps from us. Then he began his lesson: "I promised to give you the fruit when it was ripe, and now you went ahead and picked it up green. You will pay for that!"

My uncle Mohamed descended from his mule, which he attached to a nearby rock with a cord, and walked straight toward us. He reached up to his backpack, opened it, and got out a small, sparkling knife.

What was he up to? A fear gripped all of us. He asked that we stand still and not move. Then he took the melons one by one, cut them into halves, emptied each one of its pink flesh, and put a half-melon on

23

the head of each boy. Then he marched us toward the village, one after the other. We climbed the steep hill that separates the gardens from the fields of olive trees, and we ended up in front of the mayor's office in the square of the village. About a hundred meters from this office, my own father showed up. He asked my uncle, "Where are you taking them?"

"To jail," answered Uncle Mohamed, without hesitation. "They stole the melons."

"Good," said my father.

Our fear redoubled. We were heading for jail. When we arrived at the steps leading to the mayor's office, my uncle began his admonition, "I told you, didn't I, that I would give you the melons when they were ripe? Instead of being patient, you went ahead and picked them up green. They are useless. You should know that. But I forgive you. And do not do that to anyone. You can go home now." Our fear immediately vanished. We were relieved. I have never forgotten that lesson, to today.

The French colonial representative controlled the political, economic, and social life in the village. The contrôleur civil wore a military uniform. The French colonial administration that ruled Morocco wanted to have a few educated Moroccans on hand, to use as interpreters and thereby get access to the general public. With a few exceptions, the French never sought to learn the local language of the communities. They came to the country for "une mission civilisatrice," to emancipate the local indigenous people through education and health opportunities. But there were no schools in Zaouia-Cheikh. There were no teachers. Our parents were not educated. It did not matter. You had to start somewhere, and start the local French officer did.

One afternoon, while we were playing in a street on a sunny blue day in August—we were about five years old—a public announcer crisscrossed the village streets. In a loud and clear voice, he walked briskly and incessantly repeated this phrase: "All children of the village must report tomorrow morning to school, in front of the office of the contrôleur." He did not indicate the time, and that would have been useless anyway. Nobody had a wristwatch in the village. As soon as we heard the announcement, the four of us quickly went hiding in a cave nearby. But the announcer followed our movement. So, he stood at the entrance of the cave and yelled at us, "If you do not come to school tomorrow morning, your parents will be put in jail."

Needless to say, the four of us spent an anxious night. None of us told his parents about the announcement, or about the warning. The next morning, I was not certain what to do; should I report to school, as instructed? The idea of joining what appeared to us as an uncertain, unknown environment created some fear in us. More anxiety was created by the idea that if we did not do it, our parents would be incarcerated, and nobody would take care of us in our houses. Suddenly, the fear led me to make a choice. I would go to the place we called school, but what about my little neighbor, the boy who was my best friend? He and I had an easy, direct, and convenient way of communicating. It was not by telephone, or by Internet, as we do today.

Our two small dirt houses were separated by a wall that had holes of about four square inches apiece. These spaces had held the four-by-twenty-inch pieces of wood used during the process of constructing the simple mud houses, and the holes were never filled out or closed.

So the following morning, after I woke up, I went to the separating wall, bent a little, put my mouth close to the hole, and called my little friend on the other side of the wall. "What have you decided?" I asked anxiously.

He answered, "What about you, what have you decided to do?"

I replied, "I am going to school. I don't want my parents to go to prison."

"I am going, too!" he announced.

We decided to meet at the east corner. We had nothing to eat that morning, so took a piece of dry bread with us. We were both worried about what was to come, but on the way to school, as we often did, we stopped before the big apricot tree. It was about a hundred meters from the houses, majestically standing next to a creek, and bearing orange-colored fruits, lusciously ripe. We threw a few stones at the apricots, which fell to the ground. We picked them up, and while continuing on the road to school, fenced on both sides with wild-growing bushes, we took a bite of the piece of bread and ate the juicy fruit. It was a meager but delightful breakfast.

The place called "school" was a single, simple room, with no desks and no chairs. There was a mat on the floor, and a small blackboard on the wall. We assembled there, some twenty of us, all boys, no girls, all ages. My friend and I were the youngest, at about five years old. There was the middle group, maybe seven years old, and there were the "big ones" ranging from ten to twelve years old.

As instructed by our Moroccan teacher, we sat on the mat silently, but my friend and I were still anxious. We learnt, years later, that the Moroccan teacher, who in fact lived in my neighborhood, had only a rudimentary education, two or three years of schooling. He was now our teacher: tall, in a white garment called a *djellaba* and a traditional red fez hat, such as you have seen in the film *Casablanca*.

I sat between my road companion and an older boy in the middle age group. The classroom was about fifteen by thirty feet, and it also served as the court of the village. Here the chiefs of the local tribes, the wise men, rendered justice involving theft and land and water disputes, and, rarely, crimes against persons. Some children were fearful. What was going to happen? How are we going to learn, and what if you can't learn lessons? One of them, terrified, took a direct look at the classroom door, suddenly stood up, threw away his traditional *babouch* (slippers) and ran out of the class as fast as he could. I could see him continuing to run on the straight dirt road that led directly from the classroom. While he was crossing Tamda, the village river, one of the three wood panels, which had been laid hastily on the river as a bridge, moved up on one side, and the little boy fell in the river. He never came back to school. Another boy stayed away from the school for a week, and when he finally returned, he brought the teacher a gift as a symbol of forgiveness. It was a bright navel orange decorated with rows of clover. The teacher smelled the orange and gave him a slap anyway.

We were now ready for school learning. Mohamed Ould Obbad, the teacher, drew a piece of chalk from his pocket and wrote the number "8" on the board. He then distributed to each one of us a small slate and a piece of chalk. Our lesson: "Draw the number." It was not a difficult task. I had never seen slate or chalk, but I was able to complete my assignment by connecting zero over zero. The result looked close to number eight. The next assignment was much more difficult. The teacher drew a bull on the board, with its horns and tail. It was an impossible task. I looked at the board, then to my left, to an older boy who had completed the bull drawing without difficulty. I handed him my empty slate for help. He understood my request. He put his own completed slate on my lap and began to quickly draw a picture of the bull on the slate that I had passed to him.

A few months later, we were moved to another school, a larger one, newly built, and situated on the main road of the village, not too far from the village cemetery. It was close to a station where a male nurse was in attendance. In this school, we were divided into three groups according to our ages. The group of the little ones, five-and six-year-olds to which I belonged, the group of seven-to-ten-year-olds, and finally, the teenagers. We received our lessons under the same roof, our new teacher going from one team to another. This time, we had simple desks, pencils, and even notebooks, but still no books.

Two years passed, and we began to read texts on the board and copy them into our notebooks. I remember one day being able to read the large headlines on the front page of a paper that the teacher carried to class. It said something about Charles De Gaulle issuing a call from London to the Free French Army to resist. It must have been June 18, 1944, following the Normandy invasion. I would have been about seven.

All of us began to adjust to school conditions. The fear was now gone. The teacher kept us from going back home at lunchtime by offering us a piece of bread with jam or a sardine, and a bar of black chocolate.

We did enjoy these. He figured if we went home for lunch, we might not return in the afternoon.

At home, I reviewed my lessons until it became dark, as there was no electricity. After dark, I read with the help of a little slim candle, provided through rationing during the war. Moroccan soldiers were being trained everywhere in the village by French officers. Soon they would participate in the campaign of North Africa, the invasion of Sicily and Mount Casino, and in the liberation of Paris. King Mohamed V would be decorated by De Gaulle for Moroccan participation in the liberation of France.

We had little leisure in the village. We had no stadium, no toys, and no playgrounds. I remember how a few of us brought fresh spring water to French soldiers in their training camp above the Ikkor River. In return, we received a few candies, or toothpaste. But we had no toothbrushes, a fact that led to dental problems years later.

There were no sanitation or health facilities. There was only one male nurse, Khallouk, who was stationed in a shack near the school. The equipment was rudimentary. We were vaccinated for typhoid and smallpox. Khallouk used a big long needle for injection. Afterward, I had a tennis-ball sized lump under my skin that gave me considerable pain. The pain became excruciating when Khallouk, using his palm of his hand, pressed the lump hard to spread the liquid under the skin. In the summer, we saw a lot of dead people in this room we used as a hospital. They had been bitten by rattlesnakes while working in the fields. There was nothing Khallouk could do to save them.

Our pleasures were simple. We ran and played under the olive trees. We chased rabbits in the bushes. We made our own toys, like mounting a bicycle tire frame on a short stick. As it rotated, it made a nice noise. We constructed tiny cars with thick cactus leaves, connected with toothpicks, and pulled them with a cord. We collected small stones, which we rolled on the tiles of the front porch of the school. I became adept at that. My fingers are long and flexible. I have taught my grandchildren how to roll polished stones. One day, my father took me to see an eye doctor to prescribe glasses in Casablanca, a trip that took a whole day in an old, smoking bus. While we were walking in a street in the city, looking for the plaque of the doctor's office, I saw in the window of a store, for the first time in my life, a small doll. She was blond, with a blue dress and green eyes. I was powerfully attracted to this beautiful toy. I stood there before the clean window glass and admired this creature, while my father walked a few steps ahead. When he looked back and saw that I was standing still, he came to me. I expressed my strong desire to have the toy. He took my hand and pulled me away from the window, and we resumed our walk. The toy must have been expensive. It was probably destined for French children, whose parents dominated the trade and economy of Morocco at the time. But this was a great disappointment to me, which I never forgot. I knew the narrow streets, green fields, and lush orchards of Zaouia-Cheikh. We spent most of our leisure time under the peaceful old olive trees.

Sometimes I left my band of four young boys and went to sit alone on top of the hill overlooking the grain fields and orchard gardens. I would sit on the ground under an old olive tree in bloom, letting its flowers' perfume invade the air. The tree hosted cicadas, which incessantly harmonized their chants with those of others in nearby olive trees. I sat there literally for hours, two or three times a week, alone, contemplating the majestic flight of storks or the slow walk of peasants behind their cows or mules that were pulling ploughs, or listening to the murmur of the cascading Tamda river, or admiring the slow setting of the red sun behind the distant horizon. During those quiet hours, I also read aloud to myself the enchanting prose of François-René de Chateaubriand, or the poems of Alphonse de Lamartine, Victor Hugo, and Alfred de Musset. I became so familiar with those texts that I still know them by heart today. When I recited them to diplomats at the UN while I was working there, they often asked me to write them down for them. These writings described the very same scenes I had been contemplating under the tree, familiar descriptions of nature, emotions, love, and sentiments.

Chateaubriand, Lamartine, Hugo, and Musset, as well as Pascal and Pasteur became my companions. In the midst of Mother Nature's bounty, and thanks to these French writers, I developed an extraordinary imagination that still marks my life. One of those corners of nature that was dear to me was a fruit garden kept by my grandfather, Mohamed Ahizoune. He was a butcher, selling goat and sheep meat in his small shop in the village. Although we lived frugally during the war, he provided the family with enough meat and fruit for us to survive. The fruit came from his small orchard of pomegranates, figs, pears, and apricots. As a child, I slept between my grandparents on a simple mat under a blanket. And when I felt cold at night, my grandmother, Zahra Kaddour, would rub my back until I fell asleep again. As to my grandfather, each day he would wake up at dawn and begin to recite a part of the Koran, and pray, and invoke God to bless my father and bring him success.

I was very close to my grandfather, who belonged to Shab As-Sheikh, an association of elders who practiced Sufism. The elders gathered around for an appetizing tagine casserole and couscous, and drank mint tea. At the end, they chanted loud prose and poems until they reached a level of exorcism that brought them a deep sense of serenity.

Sometimes my grandfather took me to those gatherings, which created among the members a great sense of close community. I also trailed my grandfather to the fruit garden he maintained. I can still recall the perfume emanating from a hedge of wild, pink roses at the entrance of the garden. The perfume filled the air in and around the garden, and I could smell it from a distance before entering the garden. In the little orchard, I often ran after the butterflies circling the ripe fruits. Sometimes, in the summer, I fell asleep under a tall apricot tree that my grandfather was watering, only to be suddenly awakened by a ripe fruit falling on my cheek. Some years later, I went alone to the garden and saw golden grapes hanging high on top of an old pear tree. I could not resist the temptation of reaching at the mouth-watering fruits. I decided to go after them. I slowly began to climb the old tree, making sure I did not slip. I stepped only on the branches that offered some security. After about seven minutes, I finally made it to the top of the pear tree. I then took a deep breath and made sure that my feet were secure. I could see a number of hanging ripe grapes. I was positioning myself to pull out the biggest one. I secured my left arm on an adjacent branch, and then I lifted my right arm, opened my hand, and reached out for the prize. Suddenly a long black snake appeared at the top of the tree and raised his head. He was about to strike my hand. Immediately, I let myself go down with all my weight, while holding to the trunk of the tree. I was scratched by branches on the way down. I fell on the ground with my limbs and face bleeding. I had not expected this competitor to be at the top of the tree!

I was the only child born from the union between my father, Allal ben Mohamed, and my mother, Fadma El Houssain. Throughout my life, I wished I had a brother or sister. When I was a child, I often pressed my mother to describe to me a little brother who was born dead. I pressed her so hard that my poor mother had to invent a name for him, the color of his hair, and the features of his face. That description gave me some satisfaction. Another satisfaction came from the fact that I was never alone in the family. The children of our relatives were always in the house, so I had many companions.

My parents were uneducated, even though my father could do some writing and calculating, tasks required by his various occupations throughout the years. They were not opposed to education, and supported me in the long years that followed, to give me the emotional strength and determination to pursue my education to the maximum level possible.

My father's and mother's birthdays, as well as my own birthday, were never known, as there were no records kept in the office of whoever happened to rule the village. There were therefore no birthday celebrations, nor did we have any family name. At that time, the first name was followed by Ben (son of), and then followed by the first name of the father. The families were patriarchal. Men worked outside, in small trades, shops, or in the fields, and women did the cooking, cleaning, and took care of small children. There were no distractions or entertainment. The only occasions that offered joy to the families and inhabitants of the village were marriage and circumcision ceremonies, occasional fantasias (horse racing) and music played by *gnawas* (mystic music, including drums and clarinets). Men and women gathered for tea separately. There were no TVs, telephones, radios, cars, stoves, or refrigerators, or even a post office. We communicated by knocking on each other's doors. Most often, the doors were wide open. One just walked in. Privacy? Hardly. But there was a sense of strong community. People helped each other when it was necessary. Since the village had only a few hundred people, all the inhabitants knew each other.

My father had many jobs. He began by selling hard-boiled eggs, and then dried figs. Over the years, he acquired a small shop selling commodities like tea, sugar, soap, matches, candles, and spices such as cinnamon, curry, and cumin. Years later, he bought and resold wheat, corn, and barley. He got up very early, came back home only for lunch, and returned at dinnertime. He often invited friends to lunch in our house, a fact that added to the load of work for my mother. He traveled to cities outside of the village, to Tadla, some thirty kilometers away, and to Casablanca, 250 kilometers away, for business purposes. This allowed him to meet other people accustomed to city life.

Over the years, he acquired a taste for modern amenities. He was the first in the village to acquire a telephone set, in the early fifties, as well as a radio, of the Grundig type, in 1953. He also acquired a Packard car, bought in association with another man. He later went on to become the president of the local village council. Today, villagers still recall his achievements, including planting trees and building bridges and roads. He received a royal decoration for his work at the end of his presidency of the Council. He died in 1997.

During all those years, he and my mother never knew what a vacation was. In the eighties, I asked him if one day they planned to take a vacation. He abruptly answered, "Only those who receive a check at the end of the month can have that luxury!"

My mother rarely complained about anything. Her endurance and patience were legendary. She was very spiritual. Her greatest pleasure was to chat with lady friends, and years later, to see our little children, whom she adored. My parents looked optimistically on life and on the future. They surrounded me with love and, most unusual in that society at the time, they left me complete freedom and trusted my decisions. It was hard to leave them, as their sole son at a young age, and travel to

Ksiba, about twenty kilometers away, to begin the middle school. It was harder, once more, to leave them and enter a high school in Azrou, a village about 150 kilometers away. My parents visited me often. After six years in that cold, snowy city, I relocated to the famous Lycée Moulay Youssef in the capital, Rabat, in 1957. I saw them only on school vacations because Rabat was four hours away. But the most difficult time for me and for them was yet to come, two years later.

Chapter 2
Travel to Unknown Horizons

From Azrou, I traveled to Rabat in July 1957 to complete my high school education by obtaining the baccalaureate at the famous Lycée Moulay Youssef. One day in early 1958, my last year at the Lycée, a gentleman holding a large brown briefcase entered this institution and gathered us in one small room to deliver some important news. We had no idea who this man was, nor did we know anything about the message he was about to deliver.

Calmly, Shaghroushni introduced himself and informed us that he was the representative of the UNEM (National Union of Moroccan Students). He indicated that the United States had decided to grant six scholarships to Moroccan students, and he came to the school to distribute those scholarships. He passed around blank papers and asked us to write a few paragraphs in English, write down our names, fold the papers, and put them in a box he had laid on a table. When we had done this, Shaghroushni pulled six papers out of the box at random. Among the names he called was mine.

Initially, I did not think much of this development. We were all very busy preparing for the baccalaureate exams. This test is at the core of all high school curriculums, in Paris as in France's far-flung overseas territories, in establishments both public and private, and many consider it to be a foundational rite of passage. In my days only about 10 percent of the students received a baccalaureate degree, though today it is about 70 percent. When the results were announced, I earned the IB (international baccalaureate) and was contemplating filling out admission papers to the National University Mohammed V, which had recently opened its doors in Morocco's capital, Rabat.

In the summer of 1958, I packed my suitcase to return to my native village, to the unhurried rural life. I began my summer vacation at my parents' house, and once more adjusted to the simple pace of the village, unaware that the most important change in my entire life was about to occur.

A few days after my arrival to Zaouia-Cheikh, on a hot, dusty day, I began walking along the main street among pedestrians, bicyclists, carriages drawn by donkeys and mules, and children playing with balls made out of socks. As I arrived at the village bridge over the river Tamda, a *facteur* (mailman) stopped his bicycle and called my name. He then opened his large leather bag, pulled out a blue telegram and handed it to me. I immediately opened the precious paper and began to read the few handwritten lines of the message. As I read them, my heartbeat intensified, and I began to perspire. The message was short and simple. In addition to my name on top, it said, "Please report to the airport within three days to travel to the United States."

"What?" I asked myself. I was going to a country with a difficult language, a fast-moving culture, tall buildings, and pulsating lights! How could I survive the long trip and the complex life of the United States of America?

After the initial shock, I began to pray silently and to regain a calm state. I returned home an hour later but said nothing to my mother, who stayed at home all day. I waited until my father came in, just after the summer sun set. Then I informed them of this extraordinary development. They, too, must have been shocked, as they had no immediate reaction. I could imagine their agony. Were they going to ever see their only son again? What would happen to him over there? Who was going to take care of him, cook for him, and love him? Would he ever return, and when?

That night, we had our last family dinner together. The next day, I met Abdelkader Ben Driss, a friend of my father. He asked what was new. I showed him the telegram, which I carried with me wherever I went.

He said quietly, "Well, are you going? Get ready!" With his words of encouragement to me, I felt as if a new force was calling me on to meet this challenge. That night, I gathered the few clothes and documents I had, and early the next morning, my father and I took a bus that traveled from Khénifra to Casablanca, with a stop in Zaouia-Cheikh.

The trip was long and tiring. The old diesel bus made numerous stops. Inside, it was hot and dusty. Passengers traveled with bags on their laps, dragging suitcases and other bags behind them, with live chickens perched on top. Our lunch in the bus was a piece of bread and a boiled egg.

When we arrived in Casablanca, it was late in the afternoon. My father led me to the old medina crowded with small shops and bazaars. We went straight to a small, traditional two-story hotel that was familiar to him, and that had a small, traditional restaurant downstairs, with mosaic tiles. We took a small room with two beds on the second floor, went downstairs to eat dinner, and returned to our room around 8:00 p.m.

My thoughts began to race. Where was I going? Could I stay away from my parents for four years, the time it would take to obtain a bachelor's degree at an American university? How was I going to handle the language? How could I communicate with American people? What about the difficulties of cultural adjustment? Would I succeed in my studies? These and other questions agitated my mind. I was concerned that they would leave me sleepless that night, on the eve of the departure to a new world.

Two things had given me a degree of assurance. The first was the pleasant conversation I had a few weeks before with the American cultural attaché of the United States in Rabat, on the famous Avenue Allal Ben Abdellah. It was a cold day in February 1958. We had left Lycée Moulay Youssef at around four o'clock to have an interview with Dr. Francis Hammond, an African-American who had studied in Belgium. He spoke French fluently, so we could communicate with him easily. He was such an affable, smiling, and warmly welcoming gentleman, with a black

45

suit and a red bow tie. As soon as we entered the cultural section and began to take the stairs leading up to the second floor where Dr. Hammond's office was located, a wave of warm air engulfed us, as if we were entering the first chamber of a Turkish bath in Morocco. I had never been exposed to central heating. In the Moroccan countryside central heating was unknown; we kept warm by wearing wool djellabas and sitting around a wood fire.

Then the idea immediately emerged in my mind. Is this how America will be? Warm schools and shops, and no more shivering in the winter?

Dr. Hammond greeted us with a handshake. We sat on comfortable chairs before his large desk. He explained to us briefly the procedures to be followed in the universities in the United States. We signed some forms. When my turn came, he looked at me and said, "Where in the United States would you like to study?" Without the slightest hesitation, I replied, "A State with a climate like this one (Morocco), with lots of sun, and oranges." I meant that.

He said, "OK that will be California!" I was pleased to hear that promise. But another question occupied my mind when Dr. Hammond explained that it would take four years to obtain the bachelor's degree.

I thought quietly, "My God, I will not see my parents for that long!" I hesitated, and then I answered, "I would like to stay in the United States only one year, the time to learn English." Dr. Hammond explained calmly and with conviction that the studies would require four years. I said again that I would stay in the United States for only one year. He did not insist further, and agreed to my wish.

Dr. Francis Hammond and his family visiting the author's family in his native village, Zaouia-Cheikh.

47

Dr. Hammond serving traditional tea in the presence of leaders of the local Community.

I came to know him in subsequent years, and urged him to visit my parents in rural Zaouia-Cheikh. He did that. The villagers in Zaouia-Cheikh saw how an African-American represented the United States in Morocco at that time (1958). This visit left my parents, relatives, and friends in the village impressed by the demeanor of this gentleman and his family. Each time I returned to the village, family members took pride in showing me pictures taken during Dr. Hammond's visit. Knowing that my stay in the United States would last only one year, that I would study in sunny California, knowing further that I would travel the following day with students I have known at Lycée Moulay Youssef, all these factors helped me to some degree to reluctantly leave my parents, my village, and my homeland. I felt calmer that night in the company of my father in the hotel room.

Another event would keep me awake most of the night, however. When I turned off the light and pulled the sheet over me, mosquitoes began to bite my skin, chest, and legs. I complained to my father. We turned the light on, and there were very small, black insects flying over the sheet and up in the air. Each time we turned the light off and I went under the sheet, these little creatures would sting me again in the chest area, and on my legs. We finally called in the manager, who saw them for himself. He suggested changing rooms. He put us in another bedroom, a few doors away from ours, and as soon as the light was off, the stinging began again. I spent a miserable night in Casablanca, on the eve of my departure.

My father and I reported to the Anfa airport in Casablanca on the morning of July 22. In about thirty minutes, the prospective students would line up for a photo to be taken with their parents. We were five young Moroccan men, and one young woman. Despite this company, my heart started pounding again at the idea that I was being snatched away from my family, my friends, from my village and my country. I embraced my father for what I thought could perhaps be the last time.

The author, second from left, with a group of Fulbright Fellowship recipients at the airport of Anfa, Casablanca, just before their travel to the United States, July 22, 1958.

The Douglas DC-3 plane that was standing in front of us on the runway started its engines. We were directed toward the plane, and upon entering this strange machine, I sat next to the window, near my school friend, Elmostafa Mzabi. This propeller plane was heading first to Paris, then to the United States. The trip seemed endless. We spent many hours in the plane, and the day passed and the night came. Pretty stewardesses in immaculate blue suits handed candies to passengers. While glancing at the dark sky through the window, I suddenly observed that flames were thrown out of the engine on the wing to my left. I was terribly frightened. I yelled at my neighbor, "There is fire in the engine. Look!"

He calmly smiled and comforted me. "That's how it works," he said. "It's not on fire!"

At the Idlewild Airport in New York, we were met by two young Americans who led us to a small van parked outside the building. I had no idea who they were. They were dressed in short-sleeved blue shirts, with the insignia NSF. I learned later that acronym stood for National Student Federation. I will never forget their warm welcome. We had not been told that we were special students on Fulbright Fellowships.

At the end of World War II, Senator J. William Fulbright proposed a bill to use the proceeds from selling surplus US government war property to fund international exchange between the United States and other countries. With the crucial timing of the establishment of the United Nations, the Fulbright program was an attempt to promote peace through educational exchange. The Fulbright plan would forgo the debts foreign countries amassed during the war in return for funding an international educational program.

The van chugged into midtown Manhattan, where we would be staying at the Commodore Hotel (now the Hyatt Regency) in the company of our friendly NSF representatives, located at Forty-Second Street and Lexington. I got out of the van first, and one of our two companions directed me to the hotel's entrance. As I entered the building, I pushed the door, which started swinging around and around, with me still pushing with my hand. I had never used a revolving door, and had no idea where and when it was going to stop. Finally, our host put his hand on the door, stopped it, and freed me from this strange roulette. We were directed to our respective rooms, and were told to gather at the downstairs lounge for a tour of the town.

Our hosts led us down Forty-Second Street with the sun hiding behind high-rise buildings. Accustomed to the infinite vistas of the Atlas Mountains, I was disoriented because I had no idea where north and south were. As I saw blinking traffic lights and hundreds of people and cars, I felt a sense of loss and a slight dizziness. "Is this the world of America?" I asked myself. How was I going to be able to adjust to such an intense life? Would I be able to master the language? Would I be able to meet the academic requirements of an American university? These and other questions agitated my mind until we suddenly stopped on the west side of First Avenue and Forty-Second Street. At this point, one of our leaders pointed at the magnificent blue-glass high-rise building on the other side of First Avenue and said, "That is the United Nations." Our tea hosts, the personnel of the International Institute of Education, welcomed us at their headquarters nearby.

I sat in a comfortable chair in front of my smiling, beautiful hostess. She wore a well-designed blue suit. I was not sure what to expect at that moment, but my hostess made me feel so comfortable that whatever anxiety I had disappeared. She introduced herself, asked my name and country, and welcomed me very warmly. At this stage, I began to feel the American state of informality. She asked a few other questions, and when she felt that maybe I could not understand her, she reverted to French and helped me get around the difficulty of the moment. As we all left the building, I began to feel a sense of confidence for the future.

From New York City, I flew with a group of exchange students to Lawrence, Kansas. Other students were sent to various regions in the United States. Lawrence, Kansas! Why did this small town, in a Midwestern state, host the University of Kansas (KU), with a center especially designed for foreign students to learn the English language? I had a rudimentary knowledge of the language, but not enough to be able to understand and communicate adequately with others. Initially, and most of the time, I conversed in French.

The university campus was beautiful, with ivy-covered buildings of brown brick and freshly painted white trim. The foreign students were given rooms with white desks and narrow beds. Each one of us was assigned an American roommate to help us learn the practical aspects of the language. The radio on the desk served the same purpose. At night, I tuned into a station that broadcast the talks of Herbert Armstrong, from Pasadena, California. It was the station of my choice because Reverend Armstrong spoke slowly, strongly, and clearly. I could distinguish between words and sentences.

Each morning, we attended lectures that covered a variety of subjects. Needless to say, although I heard and recognized some words, most of the time I could not understand what was being said by the professors. That was not the case of the few Asian students in the program, who had learned the English language in their home countries. They were well prepared in English.

In the afternoons, we had time to view films, listen to music, or visit local sites. Late in the evenings, we individually sat with and talked to a young hostess, who helped us practice the language. My hostess, a beautiful young lady with black hair, was tutoring me with great skill and patience. Her initials were JM. Like JM, people on the campus, in the classroom, library, and cafeteria behaved toward us with understanding. These tutors had to show tolerance. The foreign students were getting the first impression of what it was to be an American at that point, and the tutors were fine examples of American directness and acceptance.

I experienced countless difficulties, mostly related to language. For example, one sunny afternoon, my roommate looked at me and said, "Would you like to go to downtown Lawrence and have a hot dog?"

I politely declined, saying, "In my country, we don't eat dogs!"

He just smiled and added, "No, no! In America, a hot dog is a name for a spicy beef sausage." Eventually I bought a dictionary of slang words, which I found helpful.

One day we were told to be ready to be flown to visit the Truman Library in Independence, Missouri. At the library, I sat next to a French student, in front of the steps leading to the upper floors. Just a few feet away from me was seated a man with gray hair, in a short-sleeved shirt and blue jeans. We were waiting for President Harry S. Truman to greet us and say a few words. I chatted for about ten minutes with my French friend when he finally said, "When is this president coming down?"

I lifted my index finger, put it to my lips, and exclaimed, "Shush! He is on the couch to my right!"

"That is President Truman?" he asked with a curious look on his face.

"Yes," I replied, "That is him." The young French man was surprised. He commented, "President Charles De Gaulle would have never come down like that! He would have come down in a military uniform, with a kepi, tie, and all the decorations on his shoulder."

This incident introduced me again to one of America's most appreciated values: informality.

We spent some six weeks in Lawrence, at KU, learning English, visiting local sights, and enjoying cultural activities. I will always remember the faculty, the cafeteria staff, and some of my student colleagues. I will specially remember my hostess, JM. The last night before I said good-bye to KU, we sat on a couch until after midnight, trying to learn as much English as possible. Her last lesson: "Can you use the expression 'do you mind if' in a sentence?"

I answered yes and complied with her request. "Do you mind if I kiss you?"

She said, "No."

So I warmly embraced her and bid her farewell. Then I remembered one of the recommendations contained in a booklet distributed to us as foreign students: "Whenever you meet an American, when you talk to him and when he tells you at the end, 'See you later,' do not expect that to be the case. Do not take that literally."

That was great advice.

Chapter 3
UC Berkeley: Center of Agitation or Enlightenment?

In the eight years that I lived in Berkeley, it was the epicenter of the spirit of the sixties. At this time, leading nations—the United States, France, Germany, and Britain—moved to push for equality for women, racial minorities, the elderly, and the poor. Thirty-two African countries gained independence. Drugs, films, and blue jeans replaced beer, dances, and chinos on college campuses. The economy of the United States was booming, and young people were free as they had never been before to drive their own cars, support political causes, and pursue happiness. The United States was growing, work and resources were abundant, and people were productive. Young people began to develop a political consciousness about national and international issues. This was more evident on the Berkeley campus than anywhere else in the country.

When I arrived, in the summer of 1959, the campus was still quiet. In 1963, when President Kennedy stepped up the military effort in Vietnam, I asked a classmate in political science if he was worried about the situation. I was astonished by his answer. "Vietnam is too far from us," he replied instantly. I was aware that, although Kennedy's ultimate goal appeared to be to disengage from the country, he was sending additional military assistance, which eventually led to deeper involvement. The Chinese support of North Vietnam was worrisome because it could be a harbinger of involvement by the great powers.

The US Army recruiting began on the Berkeley campus. Their ROTC program—Reserve Officers Training Corps—was promoted outside Sproul Hall, not too far from the entry to the campus. Students went about their business, attending classes and reading under the trees, paying no mind until protesters began to carry signs among the ROTC tables, protesting the war in Vietnam. The following year, after Kennedy's assassination, President Johnson reinforced US military presence in Vietnam. Casualties mounted. "I Feel Like I'm Fixin' to Die Rag," an antiwar song by Country Joe and the Fish, mocked the US Army.

Well come on all of you big strong men,

Uncle Sam needs your help again,

He got himself in a terrible jam,

Way down yonder in Vietnam,

Put down your books and pick up a gun,

We're gonna have a whole lotta fun

College girls joined the men's protests. Student leaders like Jerry Rubin and Mario Savio organized the Free Speech Movement on campus so that the sylvan glade became a three-ring circus of recruiters, protesters, and students like me, trying to get to class. The police were called to campus to restore order. When a former graduate-student-turned-protester refused to show his identification papers to the police, he was arrested. Savio, a fellow protester, climbed on top of the police car to address the students who watched this in disbelief. He told the students that they were just raw material being processed by the university machine. "There's a time when the operation of the machine becomes so odious—makes you so sick at heart—that you can't take part. You can't even passively take part. And you've got to put your bodies upon the gears."

His rhetoric was electrifying, and eight hundred students were arrested after thousands staged a ten-hour sit-in to support his stand. These same students passed around a collection to pay for the repair of the police car. The university responded a month later by allowing the area around Sproul Hall to serve as a forum for political exchanges from left, right, and center organizations on campus.

In the years that followed, the protests became violent and confrontational. During the era of the Vietnam War's escalation under President Richard M. Nixon, fewer Cal students were involved, and more outsiders who were looking for a good time joined in.

Even so, journalists called Berkeley the "rebel place." But that was not an adequate description of UC Berkeley. Some of us, as foreign students, did not participate in the demonstrations. As noncitizens, we had no right to do so. We passed by the demonstrators, watched for a minute or two, and headed up to the classes or the library, books under our arms, or briefcases in our hand. Very few faculty members joined the demonstrations.

The vast majority of both students and faculty concentrated on their main objective: education. This focus produced an excellent environment for both growth and enlightenment. UC, as the years would prove, produced seventy-two Nobel laureates, more than any other university. I graduated in 1960 with honors and a Phi Beta Kappa key. After two more years, I received a master's degree in political science. Then I received a fellowship to the PhD program, where I worked as a teaching assistant. I taught two undergraduate courses, one in American government, and the other in comparative government. At this stage, although I had several close friends, I again began to feel lonely. My preparation for teaching, researching, taking advanced graduate courses, and reading in an isolated small room in the basement of the Bancroft Library kept me isolated from others, so I decided to return to the camaraderie of I House. This allowed me to concentrate on my PhD dissertation.

One summer day, I noticed a pretty woman reading an old copy of the newsmagazine *Time*. President Johnson's wife was called Lady Bird, and the cover pictured her with a bird in the background. I made a remark about this strange title, and the pretty woman smiled and offered a few comments of her own.

Determined to talk to her, I learned that she was waiting for her sister and husband to arrive back from Holland and go to Palo Alto. When my two friends arrived, I invited her to join us for a swim at the university pool. We became friends. I courted her my last year in Berkeley and eventually married her.

Our courtship had some bumpy moments. I drove her around Berkeley on the back of my used Suzuki motorbike. One day, when I stopped to read a house number, a huge dog emerged from the bushes next to the house and pushed himself against my motorbike. The motorbike toppled over onto my left foot, and this incident resulted in a torn ligament. In intense pain, I hobbled back to the I House. A few minutes later, I reported to UC Cowell Hospital, just a block away. There a nurse examined me and applied ice to reduce the swelling of my ankle. Over the next few days, the nurses began to apply hot compresses to the sore area. I thought the problem would quickly resolve, but it stayed sore for over two months. Finishing my dissertation, teaching my government classes, and looking for a job, I was afraid that this injury was going to delay what I had hoped would be the beginning of my professional life. Although I had no concrete plans, I was eager to begin my career as a political scientist in America.

My original plan had been to put my knowledge at the service of my native country. Wasn't this the objective behind granting Fulbright Fellowships to exchange students, so that they can return home and contribute some of their acquired skills? I felt pride at the idea of being of service to my people. I had no idea that this hope was going to be dashed by the calculated narrow interest of the people who might hire me.

I arrived in Rabat, one day in 1965, and reported to the Faculté de Droit (Law School) on one of the main avenues of the capital. I was politely received by its dean, a Frenchman. I explained to him that I was about to complete my doctoral degree in the United States, at UC, and I came to his institution to inquire about the possibility of teaching at the Faculté. At the time, the French dominated not only the economy of Morocco but also teaching, medicine, and industry. Independence had not changed that. There were very few Moroccans teaching at the university level.

The Dean, after seeing my resume, which included teaching at UC and, briefly, at Princeton, replied in a way that I did not anticipate. He underlined the fact that Morocco still followed the French system of education. My American training was not what was needed in Morocco. When I explained that I also had a French education, he finally agreed to examine my application. He asked me to come in two days later. In that time, he was, he said, going to consult his colleagues on the matter of my employment.

Two days later, I arrived at the Faculté de Droit. The Dean sat before me on a comfortable red armchair and started to talk. He again

64

referred to the fact that Morocco followed a French system of education, but even so, he had talked to his colleagues about hiring me. He asked me if I would consider a minor teaching position, that of helping as an assistant to a French assistant professor.

I thanked him, returned to my hotel, and began preparing my suitcase to return to the United States. During the trip, I was calm. I was thinking that the French did not wish to be replaced eventually by Moroccan professors. They clung to their jobs. It was understandable. But at the same time, it was regrettable that Moroccans trained in the United States were not welcome. I was the first Moroccan PhD in political science to obtain a doctoral degree from a major university in the United States. The US government, through its Fulbright Fellowships, gave six Moroccan students, like myself, the opportunity to study at fine universities after Moroccan independence. We wanted to be of some help to Morocco with what we had learned. And yet, several of us have encountered obstacles in our reintegration in our own country. The notion of brain drain was not understood in all its aspects. International education was not a one-way street.

I returned to Berkeley and I House in the summer of 1966. By this time, I was close to completing my formal university education, and to beginning a professional life. It was hard to imagine leaving this great campus and my friends at the I House, my dedicated professors, and above all, *my* students. The Berkeley faculty was not only outstanding but also dedicated to teaching. I will never forget professors such as Edward Teller, Ernest Haas, Carl Rosenberg, David Apter, and Sheldon Woolin, who contributed decisively to my rich knowledge in physics, international affairs, African affairs, comparative government, and political theory. They went out of their way to teach and to counsel. I shall forever remain grateful for their professional guidance. I shall also always remember, with great fondness, my own students. I owe them my feeling of joy and confidence in the field of teaching. The lessons were conducted in a completely free atmosphere. They had ample opportunity to question, and to challenge, and I came to highly appreciate the sense of true academic freedom. The Department of Political Science tried to limit the size of the classroom to thirty students. I often ended up having thirty-five or more in my classes. When one day I made a comment about the necessity of respecting the limit, one young lady replied, "We like the foreign accent!" Later on, she would come to me and confess that the real reason I had more than the allowable number in the classroom was that I was known for looking at issues from a broader, comparative point of view. The day I held my last class on the campus, and announced that I would soon be leaving this great university, the students quickly began to write down on pieces of paper their feelings about my teaching. When I opened some of the papers in the classroom, I was overwhelmed by their positive remarks and by their affection. I could not restrain the tears flowing down my cheeks. I threw my arms around many of them, and said good-bye and good luck for the last time. I still preserve the precious papers.

The author teaching a course at the University of California.

Almost fifty years after, when I look back at my life of a student at

Berkeley, I would mostly retain not the agitation that prevailed on

campus in the sixties, but a sense of personal responsibility and growth,

in a free academic environment. UC and the I House contributed

enormously to my professional career, which was about to begin.

The author, center, receiving an award together with former secretary of state George Shultz and the president of the Bank of America.

I graduated in May 1967. I was still a resident of the I House at that time. Abraham Bargman from the United Nations Disarmament Division in New York came one morning to interview me in my I House room for a junior position in this international organization. The interview lasted close to four hours, and covered every aspect of international affairs. A few weeks later, I received an urgent dispatch informing me that I had been chosen for the post and that I should immediately report to New York to begin my new assignment. "Why immediately?" I asked myself. Months later, I would learn that the urgency was due to the fact that the Security Council Affairs Division needed someone who spoke both English and French to handle issues related to the then-hot debate in the Council on the Israeli-Arab war of June 6, 1967.

I received the news with both excitement and sadness. I was excited because I was about to begin work in the most prestigious branch of the United Nations. Why had they chosen me, a former caveman? I began to think of my great destiny. But I was sad because, at that precise moment, I was incapacitated. I had a cast, and my ankle was still hurting. It would be very difficult to travel to the East Coast in this condition. So, I wrote back a polite message to the United Nations informing them of my discomfort. Their reply came a few days later. This was not a problem, they said. They could wait until I healed. But I could not wait. I was so eager to join the UN. I resolved to show up for work at the organization right away, despite my injured ankle.

Chapter 4
Commitment to International Life

On a bright, warm morning, in July 1967, I crossed First Avenue,

New York, and entered the premises of the United Nations building,

crutches under each arm. I walked through the main floor, still feeling

pain in my left ankle. Even though physically I was not yet ready for the

job as I hobbled around on crutches, I felt a great moral pressure to help

the UN as a political officer while diplomats debated a resolution on the

Middle East war of June 6, 1967. I took the elevator to the thirty-fifth

floor, where the Department of Political and Security Council Affairs was

located. The administrator, a woman in her late fifties, led me to my new

office, and introduced me to my new colleagues. Later in the day, I went

to the Office of Personnel, where I took the Oath of Office, according to

which, among other things, I would work solely in the interest of the

United Nations. I was recruited at a junior professional level, despite my

experience in teaching and participating in the training of the Peace

Corps volunteers at Princeton and the University of Maryland. I could

have argued with the UN about my salary, but I let that go because I was eager to work with an organization that dedicated itself to world peace, development, and human rights.

The Secretariat building was only twenty-two years old at that point, so everything was bright and clean. After my clearance in the Office of Personnel, finalizing the paperwork for my employment, I was ready to assume my duties. Two women, Betty Whitelaw (United States), and Imogene Salter (Australia), really ran this office efficiently, with a purpose. You could not write a memorandum to them without receiving a written answer within a week.

Both U Thant and Waldheim refrained from recruiting people from their respective countries, Burma and Austria, to the Secretariat. As a staff member of the UN, I was impressed by their restraint in this area. As far as I could recall, there were only two staff from Burma, one of whom was in DPI (Department of Public Information), the other somewhere else in the UN Secretariat. From Austria, Waldheim did offer work to his daughter, Lislotte Waldheim, who was in my department, a tall, smiling and friendly young lady, and to a couple of close assistants, who worked with me at the Law of the Sea conference. This was an important consideration, because the succeeding Secretaries General would proceed to recruit staff from their own countries and from the third world.

The first few weeks on the job, I spent most of my time reading records of the Security Council and General Assembly, to familiarize myself with their work. Some six weeks after my arrival, I saw the under-secretary-general of my department, Alexei Nesterenko, of the Soviet Union in the corridor on the thirty-fifth floor. At that time, the highest official of my department always came from the Soviet Union, like Arkady Shevchenko, Leonid N. Kutakov, and Vasily Safronchuk. He stopped me and asked, "Are you Mr. Abbadi?"

I replied, "Yes, Mr. Under-Secretary-General. Do you need something?"

"No," he said. "I just remember a while ago I met with senior officials of the department. We had twelve files of candidates for the P2 level post you now occupy. We compared notes and in the end, you were chosen for the post." I thanked him and he walked away. This little incident showed me how important recruitment was at the United Nations in those days. With the right people on staff, the organization ran smoothly.

About three months after my arrival at the Secretariat, Hisham Rifai, a Syrian colleague, invited me for coffee in the delegates' lounge. It was a pleasant break after the long meetings I attended. While we both were sipping coffee and discussing issues before the Security Council, Rifai saw Ambassador Ahmed Taibi Benhima cross the lounge. He said, pointing to the diplomat, "Do you know your Ambassador?"

I replied, "No."

Rifai took my hand and led me in the direction of Ambassador Benhima of Morocco, declaring, "Mr. Ambassador, may I introduce my new colleague Abdelkader Abbadi from your country?"

I greeted the Ambassador and said that it was an honor to meet him, but he went on to ask, "How long you have been here at the UN?"

"Three months, Mr. Ambassador."

"Three months, and you have not come to the Permanent Mission (of Morocco) to say hello?"

"I certainly will, Sir," I replied. About ten days after this encounter, I paid a courtesy visit to the Ambassador. It was always advisable to know your ambassador at the United Nations.

In the 60s, recruitment for staff positions was done on the basis of qualifications, including education, language abilities, and work experience. But while the UN sought the approval of governments *after* the choice of candidates had been decided upon, candidates were recruited for skills, not for connections, in a professional and independent way. Today—and this will be vigorously denied by officials—the recruitment has become politicized, with member governments influencing the selection process.

Let me illustrate a well-known case in our own division. When I was deputy director in the Political Affairs Division, a senior P5 level post became vacant. We had to recruit someone at that level. So, on a Friday evening, the director came to my office and handed me a pile of files of candidates for the senior position, some twenty of them in total. I took the files to my country house and spent Saturday and Sunday carefully reviewing each one of them. By Sunday night, I had selected three top candidates of the twenty: one woman and two men, based on education, languages, and experience. Monday morning, when I reported to my office, I saw a gentleman sitting in the office next to mine. My assistant pulled me into my office, closed the door behind her, and whispered,

"Mr. Abbadi, that man sitting in his office is the recruit for the P5 position."

"What?" I replied, utterly shocked. I went straight to the Director's office. I had spent the weekend reviewing files for nothing!

"You gave me the files to review and select a few candidates for the P5 vacancy. I spent all the weekend doing so. I have chosen three. Now I learn that someone has already been put to work. How is this possible?"

The Director, in a calm way, replied that this was a fact. The new officer had already been given an assignment.

I could barely control my anger, but I did. As I saw no alternative to the arbitrary decision obviously made before I began to review the files, and thought that it could not be reversed, I limited myself to this observation. I looked straight in the eyes of the Director and calmly said, "May I say something?"

"What," he answered. "I would like you, from now on, not to give me any files for review for vacancies."

"That is fine," he replied.

And so it was. The P5 recruit was a Soviet citizen. It was during the Cold War, a continuing state of conflict between the United States and the Soviet Union from the end of World War II until the fall of the Berlin Wall in 1989. The conflict took shape through military coalitions, espionage, weapons development, invasions, propaganda, and competitive technological development, which included the space race. This competition between the two superpowers included costly defense spending, a massive conventional and nuclear arms race, and numerous proxy wars. Lots of trades were taking place in the Secretariat between these two nations and their allies in the areas of recruitment.

Another incident took place, also a few months after I began my assignment in the Security Council Affairs Division. One morning, an officer in charge of personnel matters in the department dashed into my office. "Could I speak to you about your assistant?" I closed my door. She sat in a chair next to me and declared, "This young lady from the Caribbean was this morning wearing a mini skirt. We never saw that here. The under-secretary-general is not happy about that."

I replied, "Don't worry. I will take care of the matter."

The next day, I quietly spoke to the young lady about the matter, and explained that the dress was supposed to be conservative at the UN. She understood. She changed her skirts to more modest garments, but in a matter of months, women throughout the Secretariat were showing up for work in very short skirts. It was the trend of the 60s.

Still another incident occurred during my first six months at the United Nations. A few days after I was stopped by Under-Secretary-General Nesterenko, a senior woman in the department met me in the corridor on the thirty-fifth floor.

"I saw you talking to the Russian under-secretary-general the other day."

"So what?" I replied.

"I wouldn't want to be seen by the FBI talking to him." She knew what she was talking about. Some nations, especially the major ones, maintained intelligence agents in the Secretariat. In this time of the Cold War, spying in international organizations was taken for granted.

When I arrived at the United Nations, the Security Council was conducting an intense debate on the recent Israeli-Arab war, the so-called Six Day War. The debate was solemn. Every chair reserved for the public was occupied. The speeches were well reasoned, rich in historical facts and eloquently delivered. The international community followed the discussions with a special attention, and the meetings went into late nights, sometimes after midnight. Diplomats of great talent, high education, and long diplomatic experience took the floor. Secretariat staff and the public listened attentively to men such as Aba Ebban of Israel, Jameel Al-Baroudi, a learned Christian of Lebanese origin from Saudi Arabia, and Lord Carridon of Great Britain. I describe their practice as "cultural diplomacy," in which diplomats worked to convince each other of their cause. Today, international discussions are conducted in what I call "technical diplomacy," characterized by give and take, a sort of trading, tit for tat.

The Security Council at that time dealt only with issues that were within its own mandate, that is, international peace and security. That meant concentrating its efforts on matters of conflicts and aggressions. The Security Council of today has a vast agenda, including sports for peace. Some will argue, of course, that in today's globalized world, everything is connected: peace to democracy, democracy to development, development to human rights, and so on. But nobody wants to admit that, in terms of the number of issues before the Council, there is a high level of inflation.

The Six Day War consumed the attention of the Security Council for six months, from summer into the fall of 1967. The Council at last adopted the famous Resolution 242 by which, among other things, the Council dispatched peacekeeping troops to the area. But the negotiations were extremely difficult.

Resolution 242 was finally adopted, thanks to what some call "the diplomacy of ambiguity." Resolution 242 stipulated that Israel withdraw its troops from recently occupied territories, but when the time arrived for the implementation of the resolution, Israel argued another way. It maintained that the text did not specify its withdrawal from *all* occupied territories. The Arab side countered by insisting that the French version of the resolution did indeed specify withdrawal from *tous les territoires* (all occupied territories). But, the Israelis and their friends further argued that the English version of the text was the original one. So, diplomatic ambiguity? Everyone interpreted the text as they wished. The resolution was adopted on that basis.

Chapter 5
My Adventure with Preventive Diplomacy

In my writing, I have used the term "cultural diplomacy" to capture the early days at the Secretariat when diplomats used persuasion and rhetoric to settle disputes. This evolved into what I call technical diplomacy, a form of horse trading, in which a party gives up something to get something.

There is another aspect of diplomacy, known as preventive diplomacy. To show the reader the atmosphere at the United Nations during my tenure, I would share my experience in the Falklands/Malvinas War in 1982. That spring, Argentina invaded and occupied these islands in an attempt to establish the sovereignty it had long claimed over them. The conflict with Great Britain lasted for more than ten weeks and resulted in the surrender of the Argentineans to an antebellum status quo. A thousand soldiers were killed in the conflict.

I was personally involved in one aspect of the Falklands/Malvinas Islands crisis. My long experience at the United Nations, the drafting of hundreds of papers analyzing the root causes of conflicts in Africa, Asia, and Latin America, led to my developing a special interest in what is commonly termed "preventive diplomacy" in the organization. Frankly, I had predicted the outbreak of a number of conflicts, and my colleagues had a qualifying term for me, "the oracle of the United Nations." I was no oracle, but throughout the years, I developed a smell for developing crises. The Falklands/Malvinas conflict between Britain and Argentina is a case in point.

Early in 1982, I sensed that tension was rising between the two countries. But the international media, especially the western media, continued for months to refer to the islands as a desert-like, rocky group of islands devoid of any resources, swept by winds, and where sheep grazed peacefully.

Anticipating mounting tension over the island, and the real possibility of an outbreak of war, I decided to take some time and devote a few weeks into researching and analyzing the root causes of friction in the area. About a month after, and some four months before the open British-Argentinean war over the desert islands, I completed a twenty-page paper containing my analysis of the situation, in which I referred to the likelihood of outbreak of war on the islands. I then forwarded it to the under-secretary-general, who sent it to Secretary-General Perez de

Cuellar of Peru. Nothing happened following that, and my colleagues and I never heard a word about the fate of the paper. In early April 1982, Argentina attacked the islands, and the world was confronted with a full-blown crisis.

Then, on the thirty-eighth floor of the UN Secretariat, in the entourage of Secretary-General de Cuéllar, someone suddenly remembered that an analytical paper was previously circulated regarding the Falklands/Malvinas. That someone did not recall when the paper had landed in the cabinet of the secretary-general, nor the date of its distribution. There were some soul-searching efforts. Shortly after, it was discovered that the paper emanated from the Department of Political and Security Council Affairs. Further investigation revealed that the paper was drafted in the Political Affairs Division by a certain Abbadi. An assistant to de Cuellar then immediately called my office. It was about 1:30 p.m. I was at lunch in the UN cafeteria. My assistant, an able but impatient staff member from France, received the call. She was instructed to make forty copies of the long paper, and to immediately bring them to the cabinet on the thirty-eighth floor. She refused.

About thirty minutes following the telephone call, I returned to my office on the thirty-second floor. My French assistant was seated at her desk, red-faced. I asked her if everything was fine. She pushed out a deep sigh, raised both arms, and shouted, "These people received the paper on the Falklands/Malvinas a long time ago. Nobody bothered to read it. Now, they asked me to make forty copies and bring them to them. I told them I am not going to do that." I tried to calm her, then I negotiated a deal with her. She would make only seven copies. She agreed to my suggestion. I then collected the seven copies, put them in a manila folder, and personally remitted them to the secretary-general's assistant. By now, the British Argentinean conflict had erupted into a full-blown war, with attacking British submarines and aircraft and Argentinean French Exocet missiles. Thousands would die.

Preventive diplomacy was never put into action, despite the warning signs, and there were warning signs. De Cuellar himself would recognize that fifteen years after. Writing his memoir in 1997, *Pilgrimage for Peace, page 358,* he said, "This dispute, long-standing though it was, hardly seemed a likely cause of war between two friendly countries, a war that would cause thousands of deaths and cost billions of dollars.

This (Argentina's claim to sovereignty) was the main reason, I think, why the international community took no preventive measures, *even though warning signals were not lacking.*"(1)

True, as de Cuellar confessed, warning signs of the pending crisis over the Falklands/Malvinas Islands were not lacking, but the United Nations did not initiate any active preventive diplomatic efforts to avert it. And when the war broke out, the secretary-general was not able to obtain a ceasefire. Argentina lost, and surrendered unconditionally. The United Nations did not suffer from the conflict, but I paid a price for anticipating it.

The under-secretary-general, at the time of the Falklands/Malvinas dispute, was a senior official at the British Permanent Mission to the United Nations. He subsequently became the head of my department. A few weeks later, after he assumed his new international functions, he called me into his office, and in an angry tone, warned, "The paper you wrote, those ideas, they don't belong to this department, and you don't either. You must move somewhere else."

I was both shocked and surprised. After a few seconds, I replied, "I respect your ideas, but I do not agree with them."

He got angrier when I said that, and when I explained that any papers I had written were approved by his predecessors, before they were forwarded to the secretary-general's office, he simply concluded, "You show confidence but you can go now. I would find you another place."

I left his office, thinking that after some thirty years in the Department of Political and Security Council Affairs (PSCA), it is the thinking of the new head of the department that I no longer fit. "What kind of thinking is this?" I said to myself.

A week after, the bureaucratic pressure began, the all too familiar formula at the UN when one's boss dislikes or wants to get rid of a colleague. My work began to shut down. I had no more instructions regarding my assignments. My secretary was transferred somewhere else in the department. I was sent into exile in the Secretariat. They tried to break my will.

Subsequently, PSCA, in the framework of UN reforms, was divided into two political departments, one run by my British under-secretary-general, and the other by another under-secretary-general, James Jonah of Sierra Leone. Jonah has been my colleague for decades. We knew each other well, and he knew what I could do. Following this senseless division, the British under-secretary-general wrote to James Jonah, asking him if he would consider taking me in his department. Jonah, a well-known international civil servant, wrote back to say that he would be more than pleased to have me as a member of his newly created department. I started to collect my belongings in anticipation of my transfer to Jonah's department. In the meantime, however, the two departments were joined together under Boutros Boutros-Ghali, and the British under-secretary-general found me facing him once again. A matter of destiny! He continued to harbor an irrational anger toward me. Most of my colleagues were well aware of this situation, including the under-secretary-general's own special assistant.

However, I resolved that I would not bend to the pressure, nor would I let the situation affect my health. Confidence? Absolutely, it never left me during my entire career at the United Nations. My background, my knowledge and experience, my meditation three times a day, all those strengthened that confidence. I also resolved to turn the situation from one of disappointment to one of positive learning.

During my two year exile in the Secretariat, I regularly visited Dag Hammarskjöld Library and did a great deal of reading of newspapers, reviews, and books, and I undertook research on several global political issues. I began writing in the prestigious Paris-based magazine *Jeune Afrique*, and publishing professional articles in journals and reviews. Those articles were regularly read by diplomats at the United Nations, and by scholars in various political and strategic institutes. Many of those diplomats began to praise my articles. They encouraged me to write more of them. One such diplomat, the Ambassador of France in New Delhi, wrote me a congratulatory letter regarding an article in *Jeune Afrique* on the reforms of the Security Council.

Although the bureaucratic pressure on me continued for a number of years, I was able to counteract it by continuing to write, and to lecture in various institutions. Despite this, I acceded to the rank of Director of Africa Division I, and subsequently, of Africa Division II. This was, to a considerable extent, due to Secretary-General Boutros Boutros-Ghali, who had learned about my ordeal in the Secretariat. But even then, I was repressed, and my level was kept at D-1, while that of my colleagues of the other five divisions was at the D-2 level.

As I was preparing to retire at the end of January 1997, the assistant secretary-general, Lansana Kouyaté, of Guinea, started to prepare a retirement party for me. I tried vigorously to dissuade him from proceeding with his generous offer. Mr. Kouyaté knew me well. He often indicated to his boss, the under-secretary-general, that his conduct toward me was not correct, but to no avail. Mr. Kouyaté and his assistants took charge of the retirement party.

I arrived at the party in the evening, about 5:00 p.m., and it was in full swing. Colleagues from various departments, including members of Secretary-General Ghali's office were there, busily chatting. Over sixty people attended.

Shortly after I arrived, Kouyaté said a few kind words about my work and experience. Then the under-secretary-general, who all this time battled me without success, took the floor and uttered these short words, "Mr. Abbadi is retiring. Evidently, he is very intelligent. We should have listened to him a long time ago. I apologize to him."

Upon hearing those words, I nearly fell to the ground. After my long exile, apologies! How could this be possible? But I took a deep breath, looked at him, walked toward him calmly, and shook his hand.

After my retirement speech, one of the directors came to me and commented, "He did all those things against you, and you shook his hand?"

"In Islam, we have the concept of pardon," I replied.

In my speech, I said that instead of proceeding the traditional way, relating one's own experience, I preferred to talk to the participants in the party about the main issues the United Nations would be facing in the future.

I listed issues such as conflicts over strategic islands (recall Falklands), such as the Senkaku/Doyeon and the Parcels, the conflicts that would follow states' extension of their territorial sea and continental shelf zones, the problems of climate change and denuclearization, and others. Then, in a calm air, I concluded, recalling a quotation from the great Scottish doctor and novelist A.J. Cronin.

"I believe that in the end, the virtue of all achievements is victory over (*I stopped a minute here*)...oneself. Those who know this victory will never know defeat."

Years later, the special assistant to the under-secretary-general would ask me over lunch to write down this passage for him. I did. I also informed him that I was able to anticipate the war over the

Falklands/Malvinas Islands because my research had indicated that, far

from being desert-like, windswept islands with grazing sheep, their

shallow continental shelf contained a strategic natural resource: oil. The

under-secretary-general passed away in 2012. I pardon him. May his soul

be blessed!

Chapter 6
A Broad View of the United Nations

Over thirty years I attended hundreds of meetings of the Security Council, first as a junior officer, then as a deputy director of the Division of the Security Council Affairs, and in later years, as a director in the Department of Political Affairs.

The Security Council is the United Nations' most powerful body, with responsibility for the maintenance of international peace and security. Five important countries sit as permanent members along with ten elected members with two-year terms. Since 1990, the Council has dramatically increased its activity and it now meets in nearly continuous session. It dispatches military operations, imposes sanctions, mandates arms inspections, and deploys election monitors.

During the years I worked there, the Security Council discussed so many topics that it would take several volumes to cover them all. As a staff member, I helped compile reports on different issues. My perspective is informed by the different angles of my work as a UN official, a member of a delegation, and, finally, as a journalist, an author, and an academic. I witnessed the efforts at reformation of the Security

Council, observed the snooping on staff members, saw the role of the UN change at the end of the twentieth century, and studied the shift from local interests to a globalized society.

The Secretary-General

During my long years at the United Nations, I have worked in the administration of seven secretaries-general. The only one I did not know was Trygve Lie of Norway, the first secretary-general. The other seven secretaries-general, Dag Hammarskjöld, U Thant, Kurt Waldheim, Péres de Cuéllar, Boutros Boutros-Ghali, Kofi Annan, and the present, Ban Ki-moon, all performed at different periods of time, and had different styles of work.

During Dag Hammarskjöld's tenure, I served as an intern in the summer of 1961 in the Department of Political and Security Council. This was my first assignment at the United Nations. The beginning of the sixties marked the United Nations' first foray into peacekeeping. Initially the prime minister of the Congo, Patrice Lumumba, asked Hammarskjöld for UN troops to subdue an insurrection there. When Hammarskjöld refused, Lumumba went to the Soviet Union for assistance. This cost him his position as prime minister. Only after Lumumba was assassinated did the UN send troops to keep the peace in the Congo, the theatre of a raging conflict. Dag Hammarskjöld himself lost his life while flying over Rhodesia, now Zimbabwe, for peace talks. The circumstances of his death remain a mystery.

Dag Hammarskjöld always had an austere air. The son of a prime minister in Sweden, he began his term as secretary-general by establishing his own secretariat of four thousand administrators and setting up regulations that defined their responsibilities. But he was also actively engaged in smaller projects relating to the UN working environment. For example, he planned and supervised in every detail the creation of a "meditation room" in the UN headquarters. This is a place dedicated to silence, where people can withdraw into themselves, regardless of their faith, creed, or religion.

He rarely smiled. He appeared quiet, always concentrating. I recall when as an intern, when I was on duty late at night, I had to deliver messages to him. I rushed up the three flights of stairs that separated the thirty-fifth floor from the thirty-eighth floor, the site of the secretary-general's office. After I handed the precious papers to his assistant, I often saw Hammarskjöld striding along the long corridor, back and forth, hands in his vest pockets, appearing worried. I learned six years later, when I joined the United Nations staff in 1967, that Hammarskjöld was very spiritual. He believed that he was endowed with a special mission to tackle the world's problems. He did not live long enough to fully carry out his mission. The circumstances of his death are still a mystery, but under active investigation at the United Nations.

U Thant of Burma (Myanmar) took over the helm of the United Nations in 1961, for two terms lasting ten years. His thinking and his actions were greatly influenced by his upbringing in the Buddhist philosophy and tradition. He was tolerant and opposed intolerance. He cherished moral and spiritual qualities, modesty, humility, compassion, and was in control of his emotions. But he also displayed courageous leadership.

I always will remember when, standing on the step of the second floor of the Secretariat, facing the Security Council chamber, he uttered these words during the Vietnam War: "This war is immoral and illegal." In the afternoon, a representative of the US Permanent Mission went up to the thirty-eighth floor to protest those words, but, a few weeks after, U Thant repeated his judgment.

U Thant believed that to be a peacemaker, one must be at peace with oneself. He further believed that he had acquired a high degree of emotional equilibrium. When he learned of the sudden death of his only son, Tin Maung Thant, on May 21, 1962, in an auto accident, he said he received the news with minimal emotional reaction. For him, birth and death are two phases of the same life process. He displayed the same reaction when he was informed that he would be the recipient of the Nobel Peace Prize for 1965.

In addition to his Buddhist philosophical and ethical upbringing, U Thant also had a personal concept of human society. He felt intensely that he was a member of the human race, and he worked tirelessly for human synthesis, through the United Nations. He admitted that thinkers like Albert Schweitzer and Pierre Teilhard de Chardin had a great influence on him. This is how he acquired the concept of universal man. He opposed violence of any kind, and worked tirelessly in favor of harmony among nations.

U Thant looked at the realities of the world from a unique perspective. He thought that the bloody disputes of the sixties stemmed from the narrow point of view of what he called the "preatomic, nation-oriented neutrality." He stated that the realities of today's world called for "a new quality of planetary imagination. They call for a global mentality that takes account of the nature of interdependence and the imperative need to change."

U Thant saw the main divisions in the world not between democracy and communism, but between "the prosperous and the abject poor, the weak and the strong, the ruler and the ruled, the master race and the subhuman." That, in his view, was the cause of tension and conflict. U Thant felt strongly that society needs to recognize the general responsibility for alleviating poverty among two-thirds of humanity. In his later years, he began to speak about world community and global citizenship. He was much praised for his opposition to the Vietnam War, intervention in the Congo, negotiations with Kennedy and Khrushev in the Cuban Missile Crisis, and efforts to settle relations between Israel and the Arab countries.

Kurt Waldheim of Austria succeeded U Thant in 1972 as a secretary-general of the United Nations and served throughout the seventies. He made it a practice to visit areas of special concern such as Namibia, Cyprus, and the Middle East. He also opened and addressed major international conferences convened under United Nations auspices, such as the Conference on the Environment (Stockholm, June 1972), Conference on the Law of the Sea (Caracas, June 1974), World Population Conference (Bucharest, August 1974), and World Food Conference (Rome, November 1974).

Waldheim was an able diplomat who tried to hold a balance between the two superpowers, the United States and the Soviet Union, during the Cold War when the UN was paralyzed by disagreements between the superpowers. He was criticized by all sides for not adequately finding solutions to the then-prevailing conflicts. He was very cautious and tried to be neutral. Yet he was a hard-working diplomat who traveled the world for his job. He was the first secretary-general to visit North Korea, in 1979. He flew to Iran in an attempt to negotiate the release of the American hostages held in Tehran, but Ayatollah Khomeini refused to see him. With Paul McCartney, he organized a series of concerts for the People of Kampuchea to help Cambodia recover from the damage done by Pol Pot. He lived for another twenty-five years and served as the president of Austria after leaving the United Nations.

Javier Pérez de Cuéllar of Peru served as the secretary-general from 1982–1991. He was a quiet figure. As the head of the Secretariat, he walked elegantly and greeted the staff with a low voice and a light smile. He surrounded himself with several advisers from the third world, including his two closest senior assistants from his own country, Peru. The head of his cabinet, from India, Virendra Dayal (Viru, as he was known to the staff), kept a tight lid on both policies and management of the Secretariat. Indian and Pakistani staff had the upper hand in the Secretariat. Secrecy (it was called "discretion") was obviously for them an important consideration in the management of the affairs during his administration.

Born in Lima, Peru, he was a lawyer by training. De Cuéllar entered his country's diplomatic service in 1940 when he was only twenty years old. In 1964, he wrote *Manual of Diplomatic Law*. After serving in the Peruvian diplomatic service in France, United Kingdom, Bolivia, Brazil, Switzerland, the Soviet Union, Poland, Venezuela, and the United States, he was appointed permanent representative to the United Nations in 1971.

For two years, he represented Peru in the Security Council. In 1975, he was appointed the special representative of the UN secretary-general to Cyprus, where he administered the Green Line dividing the country after the Turkish invasion. In 1979, he served as the UN under-secretary-general for special political affairs. He also acted as the special representative of the secretary-general to Afghanistan.

When Pérez de Cuéllar succeeded Kurt Waldheim as the secretary-general of the United Nations, he was clearly well positioned and well qualified to exercise those responsibilities from the diplomatic side, as well as the administrative one.

De Cuéllar did not hesitate to refer to governments mishandling the Secretariat. "Some governments," he admitted openly, "were not reluctant to place pressure on me and my staff in pursuit of their national interests." But at the same time, he praised the personnel at the United Nations. He believed that with few exceptions, Secretariat personnel retained the impartiality that is the duty of an international civil servant.

De Cuéllar worked diligently in trying to tackle the issues that were facing him in the decade of the eighties, including Namibia, South Africa, Iran-Iraq, and Falklands/Malvinas Islands.

Boutros Boutros-Ghali of Egypt succeeded Péres de Cuéllar in 1991 as the secretary-general. A man of great intellectual ability and enormous diplomatic experience, he was a professor and deputy foreign minister of his country, Ghali tried to steer the organization to new shores, but without great success. He was impatient and tough. He got into trouble with UN staff from the very beginning.

While he was residing in his hotel in New York before assuming his role as the new secretary-general, he was apparently advised about the negative aspects of UN bureaucracy. So, early in his term, he made a speech in which he used these strong words: "You must descend on the bureaucracy with stealth and violence." These words angered the staff union, and its members became suspicious of him.

Like his predecessors, he tried to reform the Secretariat, restructuring departments, creating new divisions, moving staff from one area to another, all with the aim of bringing about more productivity and efficiency. There was an atmosphere of confusion and uncertainty among the staff, and this "remus ménage," like under other secretaries-general before, did not bring about the desired results.

But it was in the political area that Boutros-Ghali lost his battles. He was independent and strongly opinionated, and he acted on his convictions. For example, he wanted to publish a report on the Srebrenica Massacre in 1995, but he was opposed by the United States. In the end, he did release the report, to the dissatisfaction of the United States. From there on, a psychological and verbal war began between him and the United States and in particular with US Ambassador Madeleine Albright.

The presidency of the Security Council revolves among its members each month. One day in the nineties, while I was assisting the president of the Security Council, Sergei Lavrov (presently the foreign minister of Russia), an unprecedented altercation took place. This session was a so-called consultation, a private meeting of the members of the Security Council. To my right was seated the president of the Council, Ambassador Lavrov, and next to him, Boutros-Ghali. To my immediate left was Ambassador Albright. This was around the time when the secretary-general had decided to release the report on Srebrenica, and the United States was not happy about the situation.

The topic under discussion was the UN presence as peacekeepers in Srebrenica. Boutros Ghali's reluctance in bombing the Serbs in Bosnia stemmed from French and British opposition to the tactic, as both countries had provided most of the UN peacekeepers and feared that the Serbs would retaliate against their soldiers. Boutros-Ghali looked at Mrs. Albright, raised his right index finger, pointed it at her, and said in a firm voice, "Madame, you use vulgar words!"

Immediately after that, the US ambassador's face became red, and, in a calm tone, she responded, "Mr. Secretary-General, you are the one that uses vulgar words!" Tension in the room was high. We never witnessed such undiplomatic exchange during a private session of the Council. And for a few minutes, an air of complete silence reigned. Nobody knew what to do. Nobody knew what was coming after Mrs. Albright spoke.

I had an idea that I thought would break the deep silence that followed the exchange. I was responsible for maintaining the list of the speakers for the president of the Council. The list was before me. So, quickly I pushed the list toward the president, and, with my pen, pointed out the name of the next speaker on the list. Mr. Lavrov glanced at the list, and simply called on the next speaker to take the floor. The silence was broken, tension subsided, and the Council resumed its deliberations.

As these were private consultations, everyone thought the exchange between Boutros Boutros-Ghali and Albright would remain unknown. It was not the case, however. The same day, a member of a delegation (I was told it was a Western delegation) brought the private matter to the attention of the media. It was subsequently revealed that these revelations were a part of an American campaign against Boutros-Ghali.

Indeed, from that day on, the relationships between the secretary-general and the United States would never be the same again. And when the secretary-general tried to seek a second term as a head of the United Nations, the United States closed the door against him. As a compromise, Boutros-Ghali wanted to serve for two more years into a new term, but only one year was offered to him. When he put his name for vote in the secret balloting of the Security Council, he received fourteen votes, including the favorable vote of four permanent powers.

Only the United States cast a negative vote, and that was sufficient to defeat him. But what the world did not know at the time was that Boutros-Ghali himself did not want to run for a second term. He had enough pride not to engage in a war with a big power that he knew he would not win. The real force behind his attempt to seek a second term was no other than his wife, Leah. She apparently wished to continue enjoying the prestige that goes with the high post. The information was relayed to me by a source beyond question, one that was close to Boutros-Ghali's family.

Like his predecessors, Boutros-Ghali tried, with limited success, to tackle the conflicts that faced the organization during his time. They included Cambodia, Yugoslavia, Somalia, Angola and El Salvador, and specially Rwanda. Ghali knew that a sense of confidence in the UN depended on both financial solvency and political independence. He dreamed of a professional international civil service that would not sink to mendacity. Ghali describes admirably the very problems that, before him, after him, and today, continued and still continue to erode the foundations of the United Nations. (2)

Like a magician suddenly pulling a ball out of an empty hat, the world pulled one of us out in 1997 and declared him the new secretary-general of the United Nations. For ten years, Kofi Annan would preside over the destiny of the UN Secretariat as the new chief administrative officer of the United Nations. His greatest failure was the case of Rwanda, when he held the critical position of under-secretary-general for peacekeeping operations. Like many others, he had made no special effort to stop the horrible genocide of 1994. He subsequently expressed his remorse regarding the issue.

This development was unprecedented. All previous secretaries-general came from a diplomatic background and exercised diplomatic functions, including Hammarskjöld from the Swedish Foreign Ministry, Ambassador U Thant of Burma, Austrian Foreign Minister Waldheim, Peruvian Ambassador Péres de Cuéllar, and Egyptian Minister of State for Foreign Affairs Boutros Boutros-Ghali.

Kofi Annan not only never served in the diplomatic field, he also had no political background, an essential ingredient for an official whose main mission is of a political nature. He came from a technical background. He served in the Food and Agriculture Organization in Rome, worked in the Office of the High Commissioner for Refugees in Geneva, and became the head of the Department of Personnel at UN headquarters in New York. His last function before acceding to the high post of secretary-general was that of under-secretary-general for peacekeeping operations, a function which we, in the Political Affairs Department, viewed as one of managing peacekeepers abroad.

Annan was not trained in political analysis. What is more, he surrounded himself with close advisors from technical departments. One came from personnel, another from the profession of writing novels. All the staff at headquarters knew Annan well, and some of us did work with him. As an example, we from the Political Department would regularly meet with him and his staff at the under-secretary-general and director levels, to exchange views on the conflicts raging in the world, especially in Africa. It became very clear in those meetings that the "technical staff" on the Annan side did not grasp the root causes of conflicts, and viewed them as a theater of operations, of moving troops from one place to another.

But Annan had great strengths, particularly in the field of public relations. A man of soft voice and a big smile, he greeted everyone in UN corridors, stopped the women whom he called by their first name, greeted them warmly, and asked them about the news related to their families. He was very popular. His second wife, whom he married in 1984, was a lawyer and a well-known painter. She is the niece of the Swedish philanthropist Raoul Wallenberg.

Annan's team at the UN was not characterized by any particular success in his attempt to resolve political conflicts, with the exception of Timor Leste. His greatest weakness was his lack of independence from great power politics. Kofi Annan did not show leadership during his ten-year tenure at the UN. The example of the conflict in Syria shows some evidence of his reluctance to take on serious challenges. We saw that in his position vis-à-vis Rwanda. We saw the same attitude with respect to the conflict in Syria.

UN Secretary-General Ban Ki-moon appointed Annan on February 23, 2012, as a joint special envoy of the United Nations and the League of Arab States on the Syrian crisis. His mission will be to provide good offices aimed at bringing an end to all violence and human rights violations and promoting a peaceful solution to the Syrian crisis.

Clearly, the conflict was a great challenge, and Annan's mission of bringing peace to the country was a long-range goal. Yet, barely six months after accepting this high mission, Annan quit abruptly. On August 30, 2012, he justified his decision by saying it was impossible to convince the Syrian government and the opposition to take the necessary steps to begin a political process. (3) Yet, that is what his successors and the international community have been seeking. Annan did not show the necessary patience or display the political vision necessary for the resolution of a highly complex conflict.

Ban Ki-moon was elected secretary-general on October 13, 2006, and he started his new five-year term on January 1, 2007, when he succeeded Kofi Annan.

Elected? Well, all the secretaries-general are elected by the General Assembly. But as is well known, this is only a nominal election. The regional groups propose a candidate, the Security Council makes a decision on the matter, and the General Assembly normally ratifies the decision. The reality lies in the will of the permanent members of the Council. As we have seen in the case of Boutros Boutros-Ghali, one single veto can defeat the most qualified candidate. All this is known to the public.

What is less known about the process is the lack of transparency of what I would venture to call the "preprocess process." That is, the quiet trip that the potential candidate for the post of UN secretary-general undertakes to the capitals of the major powers, prior to any announcement of his candidacy. Sometimes it is the head of state or foreign minister of the candidate who is entrusted with that mission. Sometimes the news circulates privately among circles of intellectuals or high-level diplomats. Such was the case, for example, of Ban Ki-moon.

On a clear day of February 2006, some nine months before his election, I was having lunch with a friend in a midtown Manhattan restaurant. The conversation touched on the future secretary-general of the United Nations. We both knew that it was the turn of the Asian group to propose a candidate. I suggested to my friend that there were several very qualified candidates in this region. I proceeded to list four of them that in my judgment were outstanding. My friend listened attentively and in the end said, "The candidate has already been selected."

"What," I hastened to say, "we are nine months away from the elections, and no candidate has been announced. Who is it?"

My friend, with an air of certainty, divulged the name discretely. "It is Ban Ki-moon of the Republic of Korea."

I ventured to comment, "Wouldn't China veto his candidacy?"

My friend, with an air of certainty and a smile, repeated, "It is Ban Ki-moon."

As the celebrated CBS news anchorman Walter Cronkite used to say at the end of his news broadcast, "That is the way it is!"

Ban Ki-moon demonstrated that he could face the vast problems of the United Nations while remaining a calm, respectful, and dignified diplomat.

From the very beginning, he was determined to learn the second working language of the organization. Initially, also, he did not master the art of speech-making. He was timid, his voice low. As the years passed, he showed a great improvement in both areas.

Ban Ki-moon started his work by promising to have a transparent administration and to change the culture of the organization. It is too early to pass judgment on his accomplishments, but in his eight years as head of the institution, he tackled many issues without, so far, being able to resolve them completely. The secretary-general did put emphasis on fighting poverty, humanitarian assistance, the promotion of human rights, and the rule of law. He has in particular emphasized the issue of climate change. In response to a question I put to him at a press conference at UN Headquarters, as to what was his single most important achievement, he answered that it was his recruitment and promotion of women. Nonetheless, as of this writing (2016), the crises and conflicts in the Middle East, Syria, Iraq, Libya, and Yemen remain without a solution.

One thing for which Ban Ki-moon gets high praise is the fact that he has not been personally accused of corruption. But under his administration, the peacekeeping forces were accused of committing sexual abuses on children, and even killing two young persons, in Central Africa. Ban Ki-moon was "anguished" and "angered and ashamed" by these abuses. He ordered an investigation on the issue. The secretary-general had pursued the policy of mobility in the Secretariat but that had led to discontent among the staff. He presided over the master plan, which modernized the sixty-year-old Secretariat building, but this proved to be a costly operation.

In the end, like his predecessors, Ban Ki-moon did not show a strong, independent leadership in pushing for the resolution of the many crises facing the United Nations. Rather, like the Security Council, he has relied heavily on statements and declarations.

The author chatting with Secretary-General Ban Ki-moon.

Chapter 7
Waging War to Keep the Peace:
Reforming the Security Council

The United Nations Security Council (UNSC) is one of the five

principal organs of the United Nations. The Security Council is charged

with the important mission of maintaining international peace and

security. Its powers include the dispatch of peacekeeping operations, the

imposition of international sanctions, and the authorization of military

action. One of five branches of the UN, it is first among equals. As a

young professional in the Security Council Affairs Division, as the deputy

director of that division and, finally, as a director of the Africa division, I

sat in the official and unofficial meetings of the Security Council for some

thirty years and observed its deliberations from 1967–1997.

During this time, the Security Council held discussions on

numerous questions and adopted hundreds of resolutions. In the sixties

and seventies, the Council conducted true debates, centered on issues

and questions within its mandate: wars, aggressions, and all kinds of

conflicts. The debates were solemn and serious. For the first twenty years

that I worked with the Security Council, through the eighties, Council debates were broadcast to the world. The public followed the deliberations. For one thing, the diplomats taking part in these debates were high-caliber negotiators who were well educated, cultured, and fluent in several languages. They were eloquent. Their speeches were widely read by their fellow representatives, Secretariat members, journalists, and academics. Diplomats such as Lord Carridon (UK), Jacob Malik (Soviet Union), Aba Ebban (Israel), De Rosa (Argentina), De Pines (Spain), Jameel Baroudi (Saudi Arabia), and Aga Shahi (Pakistan) debated the issues before the Council and strengthened their arguments by invoking appropriate historical facts. Their speeches were well researched and well coordinated. When the diplomats spoke, there was a sense of solemnity in the room. Attention was concentrated. If there was a fly in the council chamber, I would hear it. Today, the Council takes on a different form.

The author, right, assisting the president of the Security Council. Today, the Council takes on a different form.

Since the eighties, serious formal debates have been replaced by informal meetings. When an official meeting is held—and they are held only rarely for purposes of adopting a statement or a resolution—the chamber is empty of journalists and of the public. In place of the formalities, the Security Council issues resolutions and statements galore, without any practical effect. Many of the issues the Security Council addresses are unrelated to peace and security. The Council keeps issuing statements of warning, deploring and condemning, without any practical effect.

How did we get to this stage? Many would argue, correctly, that it is because the world has changed. There is no doubt that the world, indeed, has undergone and is still undergoing massive transformations, witnessing change at an unprecedented rate, demanding transparency at every level of government.

But this is only half of the story. The reality is that the United Nations in general, and the Security Council in particular, despite numerous attempts at reforms, have not kept up with the pace of change. In many ways, it remains an island of stability in the midst of an epoch of turbulence. But some change is necessary in order for the Security Council to remain effective. The vision of the United Nations internal structure was devised seventy years ago, at the historical June 1945 San Francisco meeting that gave birth to the United Nations. The Security Council was set up to be the United Nations' executive committee. Right from its creation, the Council was marked by anomalies and contradictions that were the result of power sharing and bargaining, especially among the most powerful nations.

The greatest weapon, the right to the veto, went to those countries popularly described as the victors in World War II: the United States, the Soviet Union, Great Britain, France, and the Republic of China. But let us look closely at this list. Was France a victor or a defeated country? Was China a victor or an occupied country? If they were not so-called victors, how did they acquire the right of veto?

One can only explain this contradiction by understanding the strategic calculations at the time of the foundation of the UN organization. The Republic of China was to serve as a counterweight to Japan, which, after the war, would emerge as a power in Asia. France would play that same role with Germany, as it recovered from the war and became an economic and political power in Europe. The other anomaly was the inclusion of Ukraine and Belarus as independent members of the United Nations, despite their belonging to the Soviet bloc that was represented by the Soviet Union. At the time, the organizers of the Security Council structure believed—incorrectly, it turns out—that the five permanent members would agree on issues before the Security Council. Their unanimity on resolutions would serve as the basis for the maintenance of international peace and security. At the time of

118

the Security Council's founding, the Soviet delegation argued that each nation should have an absolute veto that could block matters from even being discussed, while the British argued that nations should not be able to veto resolutions on disputes to which they were a party. The big five agreed finally that any one of them could veto any action by the Council, but not procedural resolutions, meaning questions that are of no substance. In 1963, the number of nonpermanent members was increased by five to bring the total membership of the Security Council to fifteen, but there has been no alteration in the basic structure of the Council. Why? One obvious reason is that, contrary to the view commonly held that the veto is a weapon in the counting of vote, the veto is actually the guardian of strategic interests. And as such, it serves to effectively protect those major interests and is therefore considered as "unalterable." Veto powers will fight to the end to preserve and keep what they consider to be their prerogative. (4)

But the Council as it exists today, based on an outdated structure established nearly seventy years ago, after World War II, is viewed by many as an undemocratic and an unbalanced institution. It constitutes the central executive organ of the United Nations. It also speaks and acts on behalf of the entire membership of the organization. So, is there hope that the Security Council will be reformed in a way that will make it representative of the international community? To that end, sustained efforts have been made in the past twenty years to attempt to introduce more representation, more transparency, and more balance into the Security Council. I have personally followed these efforts during this long period of time, and written a number of articles on the subject of reform of the Council for the Paris based magazine *Jeune Afrique*. Following my retirement from the United Nations in January 1997, I served as a special advisor for two years for the delegation of Kyrgyzstan to the United Nations. In that capacity, I took part in the discussions of a committee of the General Assembly charged with the responsibility of reforming the Council. For the last fifteen years as a journalist, I have followed those deliberations on the subject. I can testify that they are among the most difficult I have ever witnessed at the United Nations.

Twenty years of discussions, and there has been no agreement whatsoever on the reform of the Council! Two hundred sixty-nine vetoes have been cast since the Security Council's inception. In this period, China used the veto nine times, France eighteen, Russia/USSR one hundred, the

United Kingdom thirty-two, and the United States eighty-one. Roughly two-thirds of Russian/Soviet vetoes were in the first ten years of the Security Council's existence. Between 1996 and 2012, China vetoed five resolutions, Russia seven, and the United States thirteen, while France and the United Kingdom did not use their veto. The reason is clear; the veto remains the sacred cow. In the course of all those years, a number of formulations were offered by representatives and regional groups, but they died in committee discussions. Although some agreement was reached on introducing more transparency in the work of the Security Council, the two big questions—should other major powers be made permanent members of the Security Council, and should they be given the veto—remain unanswered. However, while the operational and structural details are shelved, certain broad principles that would govern the reform of the Security Council have been embraced. The Council should remain small, with no more than twenty-four members, to ensure that it can be prompt in its decision-making process; it should be transparent, so that members and the public are informed about its work. Beyond that, there is little consensus.

What is widely known is that some geographical groups hold the view that their group should have a fair representation on the Council, with the right of veto. This is the case of the African group, which is requesting two permanent seats on the Council, with veto power, and the Arab group, requesting one permanent seat also with the right of the veto. The Latin American countries also wish to have a veto seat. On the other hand, some western countries have proposed that two major countries, Germany and Japan, join the Council, with or without the right of the veto. They do not wish to modify the strategic balance in the Council. In all likelihood, no continent will obtain two new seats on the Council, with right to the veto, as requested by the African group. It would also be difficult for the Arab group to win a permanent seat with veto power, as some of them already belong to the African group, and others to the Asian group. To complicate the situation further, countries of the same size within the same regional group currently compete for the permanent seat with veto right. Such is the case with South Africa and Nigeria in the African continent, and with Mexico and Brazil in the Latin American continent.

At a minimum, there may be agreement at some point on the inclusion into the Council of one permanent member from the African group, one from the Latin American group, and of Germany and Japan. That would increase the current membership of the Council from fifteen members to nineteen, keeping it small. Should that happen, there may be some voicing dissent that the restructuring would be unfair. Why? Because, looking at the Council composition from that perspective, we would see that one continent, Europe, would have secured three permanent seats on the Council with the right of veto: France, Britain, and Germany.

No one believes that the United States should have the same equal voting rights in the Security Council as the small country of Fiji. The Security Council *is* supposed to be a counterbalance to the General Assembly. To bring the power of decision-making to a fairer level, Germany and Japan could sit permanently on the Security Council, but without the right of veto. Another way would be for the three European powers—the UK, Germany, and France—to agree on accepting to rotate the veto seat among two of them, an unlikely possibility. The other most important aspect of an eventual reform of the Council is to agree on limiting the use and application of the veto to selected vital issues.

Chapter 8
Snooping at the United Nations

In December 2013, the media in the United States revealed that the NSA (National Security Agency) was snooping on some heads of state and government, including Chancellor Angela Merkel of Germany and Dlima Roussef of Brazil. The media also included Ban Ki-moon, the United Nations secretary-general.

Snooping at the United Nations is not a new phenomenon. It began even during the birth of the organization in San Francisco in June 1945. Stephen C. Schlesinger describes in details the intelligence activities in his book, *Act of Creation: The Founding of the United Nations"*: Describing the book as "a story of superpowers, secret agents, wartime allies and enemies, and their quest for a peaceful world", he relates how the US secretary of state at the time, Edward Stettinius, had advance information of most of the diplomatic cable traffic on the United Nations from at least forty-three of the forty-five nations. This was done through the Signal Security Agency, forerunner of the NSA. According to Professor Schlesinger, the information received was of the "greatest value" to the US Department of State and to the US delegation.

When I was entering the premises of UN Headquarters at Forty-Second Street and First Avenue, the first days of my arrival in New York City, a few members of the John Birch Society handed to me and other colleagues a brochure that described us as members of an international communist conspiracy, bent on taking over the United States. And years later, some groups began to speak about the UN owning "black helicopters" with the purpose of subverting the sovereignty of the country. Kofi Annan often joked while addressing audiences, stating that the organization owned no black helicopters.

Some countries have resorted to intelligence to obtain information within the United Nations. It was known among staff members that high officials in the Secretariat, including those around the secretary-general, engaged in intelligence gathering. I was told that a senior official on the thirty-eight floor was one day waiting for a colleague from an adversary country to join him at a public meeting in the basement. He did not show up. He stayed in his office and was reading a book. The senior official finally sent a junior colleague to remind him that he was supposed to attend the meeting. When the colleague from the rival country showed up at the gathering, he tried to justify his absence. The senior official surprised him when he interrupted him and said, "I know you were in the office reading…" (He cited the title of the book.). That was how close the two watched each other.

I was a little aware of some intelligence activities taking place in my area, the Department of Political and Security Council Affairs. It should be recalled that we were in the height of the Cold War, and nations, in particular the major ones, sought to know as much as possible about their adversaries.

One day, while eating lunch alone in the UN cafeteria on the first floor of the Secretariat, a gentleman from a permanent mission of a major country sat at my table and began to ask questions about what I was doing in my work, and about work I gave my colleagues. I innocently answered his questions, as there was no secret regarding our respective assignments. I was surprised when, at the end of the conversation, he asked me if I wished to be "a consultant" for his mission. I politely answered no, and thanked him for his offer. I do not have the stomach to engage in any activities other than those related to my work as an international civil servant.

As we have seen earlier, my department, during many years and as a tradition, was headed by an under-secretary-general from the Soviet Union. They succeeded each other at the helm of the Department. It was therefore no surprise that several Soviet citizens and citizens of Eastern European countries were recruited to the department. Some of them were known for engaging in intelligence activities. Besides the head of the department, as we shall see in the following pages, there were other Soviets present in the various divisions of the department.

One case that was widely known was an affable, friendly Soviet citizen "helping" the under-secretary-general, who, in fact, had a rank of a general in the KGB. Another, in my own division, was a handsome, well-dressed, smiling man who in fact was an officer in the Soviet military intelligence, known as GRU. His office was next to me. He would close his door and read for hours. He was not reading books or reports on UN activities, but something else. We did not know what. But one day, by coincidence, I found out about his mystery. Usually, when I knocked on his door, and allowed myself in to talk to him about a particular UN assignment, he would quickly close the big volume he was reading. One day, he was urgently called by the office of the under-secretary-general. I was not aware of this event so, as usual, I knocked on his door and opened it. He was not there. In the rush, he had neglected to put the big book in his drawer. It was lying on his desk, with a title that listed US government current scientific projects. This had nothing to do with my colleague's UN assignments.

I was aware also, as were some of my other colleagues, of the day when Soviet agents at the UN would collect their briefcases and head to the Soviet Permanent Mission to the United Nations. It was always on a Thursday, mid afternoon. Those days, when by coincidence I looked for my Soviet colleagues and tried to have them join others at a division meeting, they were not there. They left no trace. Sometimes, one or two of them would not return to the office until Monday or Tuesday. And in accordance with the regulations of the personnel office, the chief of the unit is obligated to inform that office of any absentee for more than two or three days. The personnel office, in that case, required the concerned staff member to obtain a medical certificate justifying their absence. When, two or three days after, I finally saw my Soviet colleagues, I asked them to show a medical certificate. The following day, my assistant would place such a certificate on my desk, signed by a doctor of the Soviet

Mission. I then forwarded it to personnel, who had no interest in pursuing the matter.

Arkady Shevchenko, the head of the Department of Political and Security Council was an elusive, discreet man who spent many years overseeing the work of the department. A man of short height and wearing thick glasses, he spoke good English and kept to himself most of the time. When I had to report to him on activities of the Sea and Ocean Affairs Section, which I headed at the time, I found him quite nervous and impatient. My report did not and could not last more than a few minutes. At the department Christmas and New Year party, he also manifested the same nervousness, the same elusiveness. He drank heavily at the party. And when he heard that Soviet Foreign Minister Andrei Gromyko was in the UN corridor, Shevchenko would dash out of the party or meeting and go see the Soviet Foreign Affairs official. Clearly, he had a close relation with the man.

I never understood Shevchenko's nervousness and elusiveness until the day when we were all shocked to learn that his office had been sealed, and that he went in hiding. What? What was happening? we all asked ourselves with astonishment. A few days later, we learned that

Shevchenko was a double agent for the Soviet Union and United States, that Moscow had learned of his duality, and that it had issued instructions for his immediate return to the Soviet capital. Instead, he was taken to a safe house arranged by the CIA. The rest is history. Shevchenko landed in Washington, DC, where he became a "consultant" to the intelligence organization. He tells his fascinating story in his book, *Breaking with Moscow*, published in January 1985.

The press widely reported that the NSA spied on the 2009 Convention on Climate Change in Copenhagen.

It is by no means by chance that there is such interest in gathering information at the United Nations. The organization offers a central place where government representatives from all over the world gather to debate important issues. Many policies are formulated in the Glass House that do impact the capitals, both politically and financially. They also impact security and the preservation of peace. The intelligence-gathering takes many forms, from the permanent missions that house "military attachés," to the discreet agents acting under the cover of a businessman, professor, development specialist in the field, or a journalist.

Chapter 9
The World of the United Nations: Weakness and Greatness

The United Nations is by nature a conservative institution inclined to perpetuate old ideas. Sure, some would argue that the United Nations does formulate new ideas, but that is true only to a partial extent. The organization has an ideology. In the sixties and seventies, the emphasis was placed on international cooperation and on the restructuring of the economic and social sectors. In the eighties, under Boutros-Ghali, the motto was "No peace without development, no development without democracy!" In the first decade of the 2000s, the secretary-general placed the accent on the major development goals, with elimination of poverty as the priority. Under Ban Ki-moon, sustainable development took the top position on the list of issues. The priorities changed from resolution to resolution and from one secretary-general to another.

Like a tall and majestic spruce tree, the United Nations aspires to reach out to the blue sky, but can only attain a certain height due to its limitations. The organization does describe the problems well, but it does not always succeed in resolving them, and when it does, it does not find a permanent solution to them.

Every secretary-general has in one way or another attempted to reform the United Nations, without significant results. The reforms have mostly centered on issues of strengthening, and either consolidating or decentralizing, the structures of the United Nations. They included streamlining the staff and introducing a degree of mobility among them. All those measures have been carried out with only limited success. The UN, although it does carry out reforms periodically, rarely innovates. Innovation requires new ideas.

In areas of political and security policy, the concepts change with time and circumstances. Thus, the UN moved from the concept of maintenance and preservation of international peace to one of making peace, peacekeeping, and peace-building. In recent times, the Security Council has begun to underscore "conflict transformation" and "national reconciliation" as its central goals. It seems to have awaited the death of Nelson Mandela to "draw lessons" from his practicing "national reconciliation." However, even that concept does not seem to have brought a lasting state of harmony into the world. Frederick de Klerk, the former president who shared the Nobel Peace Prize with Mandela for brokering the end of apartheid, and supporting the transformation of South Africa into a multiracial democracy, has accused the African National Congress (ANC) of practicing racial discrimination in the twenty years it has controlled the country. He has indicated that that ANC regime "was unconstitutional and the antithesis to the goal of national reconciliation." De Klerk further denounced what he called the most serious failures by Mandela's successors: unemployment, education, and intensifying inequality. This shows one example of how the current UN policy has fallen short of its objectives.

Fairmont Hotel in San Francisco.

The UN ideology in conflict resolution not only shifts with time and changes in leadership, it also does not go deep into the real root causes of conflicts. Those conflicts arise not simply because of racial, ethnic, or political differences. They are born from the depths in a society where social injustice predominates, that is, in a society marked by sharp income inequality, concentration of economic power and influence in the hands of a particular group in the country, the monopoly of educational benefits and of access to administrative and military posts, and by exclusion and marginalization. In other words, conflicts arise where a massive exclusion prevails. The conservative nature of the United

Nations does not allow the organization to venture in this area. It was

established with guidelines that do not allow it to transcend the

boundaries set by governments. The mandate of the UN Charter prevents

engagement in regime change.

On July 24, 2015, the author visited the Garden Room in the Fairmont
Hotel in San Francisco where the UN Charter was signed on June 26,
1945.

The UN Charter was not born out of a revolution, but out of a war. For that reason, it serves governments rather than individual citizens. The United Nations is not an institution of the people, by the people, and for the people. True, the UN Charter states "We the People of the United Nations" but this is a slogan, not a reality. It is only a slogan, not a meaningful legal definition. The United Nations remains the brainchild of governments who exercise the power within the organization. The secretary-general is frequently only a figurehead. He does not dare to take an independent stand, and when on a rare occasion he tried to do that, as was the case with Dag Hammarskjöld, he meets with a strong reaction from a particular government. In the case of Hammarskjöld, the Soviet Union called for replacing him with a troika. There would be three secretaries-general: one representing western countries, a second representing eastern european countries, and the third representing developing nations. This suggestion, if it had been adopted, would have led to a paralysis of the organization. The governments of superpowers—the United States, UK, France, Russia, and China—lead the work of the United Nations. They exercise both political and financial influence, and carry great weight in the decision-making process of the organization.

The small states of Qatar and Fiji may possess an equal voting right in the General Assembly as compared to the United States and China, but the General Assembly resolutions are only recommendations. The real power lies in the Security Council, which is the executive board of the United Nations. Its resolutions are mandatory. The Security Council takes the lead in determining the existence of a threat to the peace or an act of aggression. It calls upon the parties to a dispute to settle it by peaceful means and recommends methods of adjustment or terms of settlement. In some cases, the Security Council can resort to imposing sanctions, or even authorize the use of force to maintain or restore international peace and security.

In recent years, a variety of advocacy groups have called for the election of the members of the General Assembly by the people, but it is unlikely that this call will be heeded in the foreseeable future. Even if this objective were realized, the balance of power would not change substantially. In the meantime, nongovernmental organizations will continue to advocate a more democratic United Nations.

A serious limitation in UN functioning lies in the fact that the organization has only a limited budget to carry out its vast mandate, a little over two billion dollars per year, not much more than the budget of the New York City fire department. Over the years, the UN mandate for implementing a wide range of goals has increased while its financial resources have diminished. In the eighties, the UN found itself compelled to resort to borrowing money in order to meet its financial obligations. Some countries have withheld their financial contribution, while others, notably the United States, paid with considerable delay. Today, the United Nations is under pressure to reduce expenses by eliminating many posts. An organization that depends on the financial whim of the member states can be neither independent nor innovative.

Over the years, also, the personnel has changed considerably. Until about the mid-1970s, the UN recruited widely from among various parts of the world. The recruitment was based on merit, including a high level of education, experience, and language ability. The staff generally felt that they were entrusted with a special mission: to cooperate together for the implementation of the organization's goals, particularly in the promotion of conflict resolution and the achievement of peace and development. They were animated by the ideals of the UN Charter and encouraged by senior officers. Their files were reviewed periodically by a peer of senior colleagues and their promotions were predictable, based on merit and achievement. The process was open and transparent. The staff felt proud to have been chosen among hundreds of candidates for a unique profession. Cooperation within and between departments was the rule. A spirit of team prevailed, and morale was high.

Since then, the life of the international civil servant has changed. It has clearly and unmistakably deteriorated. Any objective observer would testify to that, including the staff themselves, but the top managers will naturally continue to deny the facts.

What has happened, and why? The situation is the result of a variety of factors, including in particular the following:

The number of posts available in the Secretariat has diminished and with it, the opportunities for promotion. There are fewer jobs at the United Nations, and fewer employees, even talented ones, have opportunities to move up in the UN organization.

But the overriding reason for the low staff morale today lies in the politicization of the recruitment process. I remember the days when members of delegations were genuine when they promised not to interfere in the internal affairs of the UN staff. Indeed, governments limited themselves to recommending candidates to the high political positions of assistant secretaries-general and under-secretaries-general.

Today, in many cases, governments involve themselves in the recruitment process of even junior officers. As the head of several sections and divisions in the Secretariat, I have witnessed firsthand the corruption of the process. This included the intervention of members of the cabinet of the secretary-general as well as that of the heads of departments. Some of them initiated the practice of lending a vacancy in their department to their counterparts in another department, to enable their favorite candidate to obtain a promotion. The favor was returned at the appropriate time. Trading took the place of appointing by merit or promoting through achievement. Some high officials were quick to promote the staff with whom they had personal relations. These staff favorites jumped from mid professional levels to assistant secretaries and under-secretaries-general in no time. Joking about that, some embittered staff members noted that the appointees' favorites took the elevators, while the rest of the staff had to take the stairs. This unfairness

generated a sense of frustration among the staff.

One consequence of such a situation is the decline in some staff's

commitment, enthusiasm, and devotion to the tasks of international civil

servants. In some cases, the staff seem to have lost any hope in the

improvement of their lot. As one of them confided to me over lunch in

the cafeteria, "I am just hanging on, waiting for the day of my retirement.

I am no longer going to kill myself at work, and frankly, I don't care

anymore."

This situation is not terminal. It can be redressed if fair measures are

instituted regarding both recruitment and promotion. The promotion and

recruitment boards that are already in place require revitalization.

Members of these boards with special links to heads of department, for

whom they render favors and special assistance, should be replaced by

professionals with transparent policies.

The time has come to remedy this situation, to appoint a small,

independent commission with wide geographical representation to

advise on the issues. The members should have the necessary experience

in the human resource field, and be chosen on the basis of their integrity.

I have suggested that procedure in a letter to Kofi Annan following his election as a secretary-general in 1997. He chose to ignore the recommendation. The recruitment process, if undertaken correctly, constitutes a crucial step in providing the Secretariat with an army of dedicated and committed men and women who form the core of international service and who exercise their responsibilities solely in the service of the United Nations. A perverted recruitment and promotion system, based on personal relations and favoritism, would provide the Secretariat with cadres of mediocre quality, a situation which would impact their performance.

Implementation of clear standards of language and experience, and promoting those who show initiative and proactivity, will make the UN more effective, and member countries can take pride in the work that this organization does, with staffing from all over the world.

Chapter 10
Idealism and Strength

In the last chapter, I pointed out some of the limitations of the United Nations, but there is another aspect that bears examination as well: its accomplishments. The United Nations is an experiment in international cooperation. It is only seven decades old, and yet, during this relatively short period of its history, it has achieved much.

When I joined the United Nations in 1967, it was not because of the salary it offered me. It was relatively low, and I did not negotiate it. Rather, I took the job because I embraced an ideal of hope. During the first weeks of working at the United Nations, I read the Charter over and over. The authors of the UN Charter offered a vision for the future of humanity that could leave no man or woman indifferent. As a charter, it is a constituent treaty, and all members are bound by its articles. Furthermore, Article 103 of the Charter states that obligations to the United Nations prevail over all other treaty obligations.

"We the Peoples of the United Nations," the Charter states at the very beginning, "determined to save succeeding generations from the scourge of war...to reaffirm faith in fundamental human rights, in the dignity and worth of the human person, in the equal rights of men and women and of nations large and small...to promote social progress and better standards of life in larger freedom..."

This introduction to the Charter says it all. It expresses the ideals to which humanity is ascending as it progresses through long, difficult, and often tortuous stages. Keeping faith in those ideals, one cannot lose hope. Forgetting them, one can easily experience frustration and possibly even hopelessness. French scientist and philosopher Blaise Pascal said that *"L'homme n'est ni ange ni bête"* ("Man is neither angel nor a beast"). Because the United Nations works toward an ideal, it leads men to righteousness, by working through the ordinary reality of the world. Since the world is in the midst of unprecedented transformations, the United Nations itself, as an institution, must move along with the times. As these transitions persist, the United Nations is bound to undergo profound changes. The question is therefore whether it will be able to evolve as the world evolves, or whether it will become irrelevant to the point of knowing the same fate as that of its predecessor, the League of Nations.

Yet it cannot be denied that the United Nations has many accomplishments. It has not saved succeeding generations from the scourge of war. But it has put off the flames of conflict in many areas of

the world, particularly in Africa, including Burundi, the Congo, Liberia,

Sierra Leone, Mozambique, and Angola. It has also contributed to

stability in Mozambique, Namibia, and South Africa. It has failed to stop

genocide in Rwanda. The United Nations has sacrificed many soldiers in

other areas, as well as its own staff. These deaths show us that the

United Nations still has much to learn about conflict resolution around

the world.

The UN has been more successful in the process of the

decolonization of many countries. After World War II, the United Nations

was instrumental in putting the necessary international pressure on

countries holding colonies to facilitate access to independence of those

colonies.

The United Nations played an important role in the elimination of

apartheid in South Africa. The elimination of this system of legalized

racial discrimination was on the agenda of the United Nations from its

inception. On June 22, 1946, the Indian government requested that the

discriminatory treatment of Indians in the Union of South Africa be

included on the agenda of the very first session of the General Assembly.

In the decades that followed, the world body would contribute to the global struggle against apartheid by drawing world attention to the inhumanity of the system, legitimizing popular resistance, promoting anti-apartheid actions by governmental and nongovernmental organizations, instituting an arms embargo, and supporting an oil embargo and boycotts of apartheid in many fields.

Another overlooked area of achievement lies in the vital work undertaken on a daily basis by what is termed the "UN system." This system includes, among others, the World Bank, International Monetary Fund (IMF), World Health Organization, International Telecommunication Union, World Meteorological Organization, Universal Postal Union, United Nations Children's Fund (UNICEF), United Nations Educational, Scientific, and Cultural Organization (UNESCO), etc.

The United Nations is a unique organization. It is the only truly global organization where world leaders meet each year, under the same roof, to examine the world's problems and exchange views on their solutions. Critics claim the United Nations is only a debating society where the issues are discussed but not resolved. It takes an enormous amount of time for an organization as large and as multifarious as the

United Nations to complete any task once it has been set. Add to that the weeks and months that negotiations require, and anyone's patience runs out. In matters like the Tutsi genocide in Rwanda, or the Indonesian occupation of East Timor/Timor Leste, where hundreds of thousands of people died, this criticism seems justified.

But the question of the United Nations' effectiveness can be examined more productively from another angle. Of course it takes time for 193 countries to reach an agreement. The appointed representative of every country must explain and argue the position of his or her country freely and without restriction. The question therefore can be reversed: how can one expect 193 countries to come to agree on anything at all? Yet, surprisingly, they do agree most of the time, despite the diversity of views.

Photo of the author chatting with US Ambassador Zalmay Khalizad.

The Security Council's activities are scrutinized more closely than those of the many UN institutions because that is where the real power lies. The Security Council addresses issues of war and peace. Reaching consensus in the Council with its fifteen members—five permanent and ten non permanent—is not an easy task. Nations do not compromise easily on their core interests. There was a time during the Gorbachev-Reagan era when it was thought that consensus within the Security Council would be reached more easily, but that was a temporary illusion.

I postulate that the United Nations will be able to achieve a higher level of effectiveness in the twenty-first century world only if it is transformed profoundly, reflecting the changes that are taking place in the world around it. In the past, it has moved forward with occasional piecemeal reforms. The United Nations, if it is to survive and thrive, must reflect the realities of our world. Furthermore, the secretary-general should push for more equality between men and women in the Secretariat. I suggest that the secretary-general, if a man, recommend to the General Assembly the election of a woman as the deputy secretary-general.

In this way, the United Nations could bring its constitution—the Charter—in line with today's realities. It is paradoxical that the United Nations unwillingly violates its own constitution. A clear example is Article 2, Paragraph 7, which states that "nothing contained in the present Charter shall authorize the United Nations to intervene in matters which are essentially within the domestic jurisdiction of any state." Despite this restriction, the United Nations today interferes with those internal matters. The organization today oversees elections, and assists in the drafting of constitutions. Much good results from these interventions, so the Charter should be revised to acknowledge that this is part of the United Nations mandate.

The author (right) chatting with the ambassadors of Cyprus, Andreas Jacovides (Left) and Fiji, Satya Nandan (Center).

Elsewhere, the United Nations often praises itself for inventing the system of peacekeeping, which it proudly and hastily says is not a part of the Charter. Clearly, this is another paradox. How can the organization claim to stick to the clauses of its charter, and at the same time operate freely outside of it?

Further, the Charter, in its Article 47, Paragraph 1, establishes a Military Staff Committee to advise and assist the Security Council. It consists of the chiefs of staff of the permanent members of the Council. The Committee is responsible for the strategic direction of any armed forces placed at the disposal of the Security Council. This important function is never implemented in modern peacekeeping operations.

In Articles 108 and 109, the Charter lays out procedures for amending the Charter through a general conference of member states. No such meeting of member states has ever been held. Why is the United Nations violating its own basic law? If the United Nations were to begin amending the Charter that would certainly open a Pandora's box. There would be calls for changes in many provisions of the Charter. And yet, an organization that purports to reflect the ideals and aspirations of humanity of succeeding generations should anticipate changes and lead the world in that direction.

CHAPTER 11
The United Nations in the World of Tomorrow

The second secretary-general, Dag Hammarskjöld, advised,

"Never look down to test the ground before taking your next step; only

he who keeps his eye fixed on the far horizon will find the right road."

The UN already promotes ideals of global citizenship—as

exemplified by the celebrity ambassadors who represent UN specialized

agencies, such as Vern Yip and Marcus Samuelsson for UNICEF, Princess

Lalla Meryem of Morocco and Omer Zaifu Livaneli for UNESCO. The global

institutions that stand alongside the United Nations like the World Bank

and the International Court of Justice have provided us with ways of

working on a global basis. Continuing with this Big Picture approach to

world problems will require flexibility on the part of the United Nations

itself, as well as its individual members.

The UN Charter is the supreme treaty in the world. All members

are bound by its articles. Furthermore, Article 103 of the Charter states

that obligations to the United Nations prevail over all other treaty

obligations. Yet, it is not perceived that way at present. That is because

we are in the midst of a long transition.

The forces of globalization are at work during the transition: technology, trade, the World Wide Web, social media, interconnected financial institutions, tourism, and migration, etc. They all add their brick to the edifice of globalization, to the structures of the world community. Day after day, citizens of the world find themselves exposed to and affected by the values of others, in different lands. The chain of other's hopes and aspirations develops links to theirs. The civil society in one country begins to share the concerns of those in other countries. Communication between them strengthens. A feeling of fraternity, of brotherhood and sisterhood is being born, particularly among young people. They extend their hand to each other across the oceans and continents. Compassion develops. And a sense of human solidarity is now slowly taking shape before our own eyes.

Amid a rapidly changing old world marked by divisive and contradictory currents, there is an emerging new world, characterized by common and unifying dimensions. We are transitioning from the stage of international relations to the stage of global partnership. The age of global partnership will require profoundly restructured institutions or new global institutions altogether. Secretary-General Boutros Boutros-

Ghali warned nearly twenty-five years ago that no state could escape the revolutionary changes in international systems. Not only were old ideas being replaced by new ones, these new ideas were influencing the way governments operated and people conducted their daily business. While these changes can bring a fresh perspective and new efficiencies, they can also create disruptive violence. International organizations like the United Nations must commit themselves to a costly and difficult process of adjustment to these new global ways.

The requirement of the twenty-first century—the establishment of a global partnership—will be preceded by a process of deepening consciousness about human values. I review these values in a chapter in the book titled *Vision for a New Civilization*. (5) Others have more recently spoken or written about those values, including Nicolya Christi who in her work, *Contemporary Spirituality for an Evolving World*, has said that a seismic shift will be required to ensure the well-being of both the individual and the collective in the future. She recommends that we move from consumerism to humanitarianism to improve every life on the planet. A move from consumerism to humanitarianism would be required at every level of policy, in every country in the world. (6)

The voice of people, as individuals as well as in groups, has been rising for years, just like the temperatures in the oceans. In the twenty-first century, the stress has been on income inequality, and social injustice. This is the new consciousness, arising from every corner of the world. Some prominent spiritual leaders have begun to raise the moral aspect of the issue. Pope Francis writes as follows:

"We do not need plans drawn up by a few for the few, or an enlightened or outspoken minority which claims to speak for everyone. It is about agreeing to live together, a social and cultural pact."

Pope Francis further shows how inequality and exclusion are linked to violence. "Until exclusion and inequality in society and between peoples is reversed," he states, "it will be impossible to eliminate violence."

He pursues the point:

"When a society—whether local, national or global—is willing to leave a part of itself on the fringes, no political programs or resources spent on law enforcement or surveillance systems can indefinitely guarantee tranquility."

The Pope finally concludes his thinking on the issue this way: "Inequality eventually engenders violence, which recourse to arms cannot and never will be able to resolve." (7)

These important thinkers and theologians show us how the United Nations needs to adapt itself if it is to survive. It must undertake the profound reforms appropriate for the advent of the Global Partnership, and to add to its agenda, as a high priority, the issue of social justice. The UN will have to streamline its bloated agendas, and as private industry has done, return to the core issues by shedding related, but minor, items. A prime example of this is the Security Council, which deals today with matters that are not directly related to peace and security such as mine crystallization. I am talking about guerrilla groups in those countries that sell precious metals to buy arms.

I know from personal experience that limiting the issues the Security Council examines is not an easy undertaking. The Council could assign some issues to the General Assembly and its Committees, to the

Economic and Social Council, and to appropriate United Nations agencies, such as the International Labor Organization (ILO) and Food and Agriculture Organization (FAO) when the matters under discussion are not threatening peace and security. The Council, for example, does not have to deal with subjects such as sports or mine crystallization. It should concentrate its attention on issues truly threatening international peace and security, such as mounting tension or aggression, not on peripheral ones, which are essentially of an internal nature to nation states.

As we discussed in chapter 7, reforming the Security Council has been a top priority of the United Nations for over twenty years. But even if the UN included Germany, Japan, and others as permanent powers of the Security Council (with or without the right of veto), this measure would not substantially change the balance of power within the Security Council.

What would?

I have pondered this question during long years of work in the Security Council. I believe that a more equitable representation on the Security Council would, in the long run, be realized on a geographical basis. This is not for tomorrow, I am aware. But in the age of global partnership, a permanent seat with veto right to each major region (Africa, Asia, Western Europe, Eastern Europe, North America, and Latin America) would bring more equality by limiting the number of members to only fifteen or sixteen. I am aware also of the fact that states within Europe who now hold the veto power would not want to relinquish that privilege. As will be recalled, history has also shown that nations are always reluctant to abandon their control, whether it is over colonies or in a state of occupation.

In that context, the United Nations, in the era of global partnership, can begin to approach the issues of war from different perspectives. One way of looking at the subject is to consider sub regional and regional integration in every continent. By working consistently and directly on the objective of integration of continents, the organization would avoid intervening in every domestic conflict. This would save resources as well as the lives of the peacekeepers.

Toward that objective, the United Nations would assist in drawing up plans for sub regional and regional integration where they don't exist. Where they already exist, the United Nations could provide the necessary technical, financial, and technological resources toward a smoother integration.

Similarly, the international financial institutions in the era of global partnership should be restructured to reflect more geographical representation. Both the International Monetary Fund (IMF) and World Bank were created in the aftermath of World War II to help stabilize world finance. In 1947, they became specialized agencies of the UN. They report to the Economic and Social Council (ECOSOC) and participate in many UN meetings. The head of the IMF, or managing director, was always a European; the head of the World Bank, or president, was always American. The head of the IMF is now French. The head of the World Bank is now a Korean. The IMF is concerned with the whole world, while the World Bank is focused on developing countries. The IMF gives large loans, in the hundreds of millions and billions, whereas the World Bank gives smaller loans, in the tens of millions, for specific projects like dams or oil pipelines.

The IMF was created with a goal to stabilize exchange rates and supervise the reconstruction of the world's international payment system. Countries contributed to a pool that could be borrowed from, on a temporary basis, by countries with payment imbalances. It is an organization of 185 countries working to foster global monetary cooperation, secure financial stability, facilitate international trade, promote high employment and sustainable economic growth, and reduce poverty. With so-called mission creep, the IMF is now making smaller grants, once the exclusive sphere of the World Bank.

There are no overriding reasons why the IMF and the World Bank should not form as a single global financial institution. The same can hold for the World Trade Organization (WTO) and United Nations Industrial Development Organization (UNIDO). World Trade Organization Director-General Supachai Panitchpakdi maintained that when it came to technical assistance and capacity building, strengthening capacities to implement WTO rules was not enough. Success will only come through result-oriented coordination with other agencies, like UNIDO, with the mandate to assist with the development of the productive capacities of industry. This is an example of moving toward better integration of specialized economic development agencies in order to guarantee more efficiency and wide geographical representation.

The new motto of the United Nations should be *Peace and Development through Integration*. Historically, the states that have formed a union or a federation as Europe or the United States have done, do not declare war on each other, because they have common interests. Those interests are greatly enhanced by the union. Union enhances the prospects for peace and opens possibilities for prosperity.

A real debate on regional integration should begin at the highest level at the United Nations, at a planned summit of heads of state and government. Resources should be transferred to a higher level from the piecemeal micro-approach of peacemaking and peacekeeping.

Equally, the United Nations should make preventive diplomacy one of its core goals, and not a side issue as it is today. Once financial resources are made available to underwrite the transition to emphasizing preventive diplomacy, the Security Council should serve as a regular, active center for discussing preventive diplomacy and its use where it is needed. UN members who are party to conflicts, actual and potential, should be invited to appear before the Council and describe their grievances, and the Council should make concrete recommendations to the parties to the conflict. This is not the case today, when, as we have

162

seen, the Security Council spends time issuing presidential statements and declarations.

The United Nations, as seen above, often cites these important words of its charter, "We, the People of the United Nations." Unfortunately, the organization cannot serve as a model of democracy. Nor can it democratize itself. Governments will never do that. Instead, it is up to individuals to exert their influence to open up the United Nations. People, not governments, will bring more democratic measures into the United Nations structures and operations. Civil society is attempting to do that.

To make it easier for individual citizens and advocacy groups to be heard, the secretary-general should go beyond the global compact. I would recommend establishing a global partnership that could be composed of representatives of the regional groups that make up the United Nations. Each group would send six representatives from its private sector, eight representatives of the region's NGOs (nongovernmental organizations), including two representatives who advocate the rights of children and women, and three from the region's religious community. These representatives would provide the secretary-general with informal advice on the priorities of the United Nations.

The world has begun recently to witness the first signs of new regional integration and new world cooperation. The secretary-general, Ban Ki-moon, has emphasized that group effort is essential in realizing the goals of the United Nations. He has said that the secretary-general, or even the United Nations with all its members, cannot do it alone. The United Nations needs support from business, religious, philanthropic, and military leaders to solidify our political will. Working together, all these segments of society can mobilize resources that can be used as tools for peace and security.

That is why Ban Ki-moon recommended to the General Assembly: "Let us have some more structured way of mobilizing this support from all member states. I have proposed this as a form of a global partnership facility." Already, regions are aligning their interests to represent the common concerns of a given area. Ten African nations formed a new African group in 2014, after the failure to resolve the conflict in Mali and the Central African Republic. The African Capacity for Immediate

Response to Crises includes an effort to accelerate the creation of an African rapid reaction force to deal with crises. Such a force would be set up voluntarily to intervene in specific cases by the African Union's Peace and Security Council.

It took ten years for the countries to take this great concept into practice. Among the countries contributing to the force are Uganda, Tanzania, Ethiopia, Mauritania, Algeria, Angola, South Africa, Guinea, and Chad. This action demonstrates the willingness of African states to ensure their independence in military matters. Not all African leaders are in favor of this extraordinary measure, but it constitutes a beginning in the taking of independent free initiative in the continent of Africa. The action certainly inaugurates a new development in the willingness of a regional organization to assume its own responsibility for regional security.

The second example can be seen in the decision of some thirty states from diverse continents to launch the foundations of a global cooperation in the space exploration of the universe. They include the United States, China, Russia, Japan, India, and Brazil. These countries and others have left aside their rivalries to engage in the joint exploration of space. The United Nations Office for Outer Space Affairs was initially

165

created as a small expert unit within the United Nations Secretariat to assist the ad hoc Committee on the Peaceful Uses of Outer Space established by the General Assembly in 1958. It became a unit within the Department of Political and Security Council Affairs in 1962.

It is self-evident that wars are expensive. Global cooperation, underpinned with a strategy of preventive diplomacy, can help resolve global problems as an alternative to war. We can no longer dismiss the capacity of states to form a true United Nations, and to unite their efforts toward the peaceful settlement of disputes, conquest of poverty, and conclusion of peace. The era of global partnership offers win-win solutions, which benefit individuals as well as nations.

Chapter 12
Special Missions and the Stories Accompanying Them
The Panama Canal Referendum

From time to time, the United Nations calls on its staff to undertake special missions overseas. That consists in attending conferences away from UN headquarters, participating in the supervision of national elections, or representing the secretary-general at important events abroad. I was privileged to take part in some of those missions. As its title implies, my department, the Department of Political and Security Council Affairs, dealt with issues before the Security Council, the most important body of the United Nations. It was therefore considered crucial that officials working on Security Council matters related to this be included in the special missions.

During the term of President Jimmy Carter, a referendum was planned for deciding whether the Panama Canal, which was under US administration, should revert back to Panama. The United Nations set up a team of six specialists to form an observer mission to supervise and verify the elections, headed by a UN under-secretary-general from Belgium, Erik Suy. There were three members from the Office of Legal

Affairs. I was appointed to represent the Department of Political and Security Council Affairs. Our team was accompanied by two officers from the UN Security Services. George Illueca, Panama's UN ambassador, a gentle and anxious diplomat, flew with us from New York to Panama. At that time, the country was ruled by General Omar Turrijos, who was viewed as a dictator. But we never would meet the general. We were told he had left the country. The implication was clear: General Omar Turrijos would not interfere in the process of the United Nations referendum on the reversion of the management of the Panama Canal.

We arrived at the airport in Panama City on October 19, 1977. After a quick meeting with Panama officials, we studied the voluminous documentation we brought with us from New York, including geographical maps, population density charts for various areas of the country, the organization of the referendum, the structures of the nongovernmental organizations in Panama, and the position of army barracks. Most important for UN observers, we familiarized ourselves with the geography of the area we would be monitoring, and the location of its polling stations. Then we divided ourselves into three teams, to cover the three regions of the country. I was assigned to the region of

168

Bocas Del Toro, where the mayor of one of the villages met me with a big bag of bananas. Since UN regulations do not allow for individual gifts, I had to decline them. Then he offered to take me in his car to the place where I was supposed to observe the elections. I had to decline this offer as well, since the UN had provided me with a car, a driver, and a helicopter of my own. We drove to a neighboring city and boarded a noisy black helicopter. I sat in the back of the helicopter. The place I was to observe was a small area located between high mountains. The helicopter flew over them, and then started to dive, shaking terribly. Below us was a narrow river, with a bridge in the middle. As the helicopter was now flying low, slowly, toward the bridge area, I could see two long lines of people who appeared to be school children, lining up on the other side of the riverbank, and proceeding to vote. Immediately, in a simple Spanish language, I said to the pilot loudly, "*Los niños no pueden votar!*" ("Those children cannot vote!") He simply smiled, and ignored my observation. I repeated my remarks. He took off his earphone, looked back at me with a smile, and said, "*No son niños!*" ("They are not children!") A few minutes after the pilot landed the helicopter, just before the bridge, I jumped out, crossed the bridge, and walked toward the two long lines. The pilot was correct, they were not children. Some of them looked old enough to be grandparents. They were the pygmies of the region. These people came from far, walking literally hours in difficult terrains, toward this polling station, in order to exercise their right to vote. I had nothing but admiration for them.

We observed the voting all day. At the end, I accompanied the ballot boxes back to their destination in the capital of the mountainous regions. The process was orderly, without any interference from the army. We had previously interviewed a cross section of local citizens: journalists, lawyers' associations, students' associations, trade union leaders, teachers, and business leaders. Aside from a few anomalies, like some voting boxes without curtains, the election was peaceful. The outcome was a democratic expression of the people's wishes: two-thirds for, one-third against. The Panama Canal Treaty was abrogated. Ambassador George Illueca, always a little anxious, could at last relax. The United Nations received a report from the team, which brought out the results of the referendum, a report that the UN General Assembly endorsed as an official document.

The Arab Summit of 1982

UN Secretary-General Kurt Waldheim received an invitation to attend the summit of the leaders of the Arab countries from September 6-9, 1982, in Fes, Morocco. His heavy schedule at the time, however, did not allow him to make the trip. Instead, he appointed a delegation to represent him at the summit. It included Abby Farah, the under-secretary-general of the Department of Trusteeship and Decolonization (Somalia), Ismat Kittani, chef de cabinet (Iraq), and me (Morocco). My job was to assist Abby Farah by translating the Arabic language that would be spoken at the summit.

We arrived at Seis airport in Fes. As we descended the steps of the airplane, Abdel Haq Tazi, the Moroccan secretary of state for foreign affairs, shook hands with Abby Farah, then with Ismat Kittani. When I was a step from him, he totally ignored me. We proceeded to the beautiful Royal Palace in Fes, located in a green environment. At the entrance, security was heavy. We had to wait for a long time to receive our badges. Then we walked together to the gate of the Royal Palace. At the gate, security services checked Abby Farah's badge, and let him enter the premises. Then they examined Ismat Kittani's and let him cross the gate.

When my turn came, the security officer at the gate refused to let me in. I was Moroccan! Abby Farah was led to his seat on the main floor as an observer from the UN. I was still outside the gate to the entrance to the Royal Palace when an old friend, a former member of the Moroccan Mission to the UN, now in the Ministry of Foreign Affairs, saw me, pulled me by hand toward the gate and told the security officer: "He is from the UN, I know him." He then looked at me and said, "Please proceed." But it was too late.

The damage had been done. Abby Farah had looked back to see if I was seated behind him. He saw that all the seats were occupied by others. I had been taken to an empty seat on the second floor, from which I listened to the speeches. When, hours later, the meeting ended, I explained to Farah what had happened. Farah had been assigned by the secretary-general to discuss the question of the Sahara with Moroccan authorities in Fes, a conflict that was raging at the time. Farah wanted to speak to the Moroccan foreign minister, M'hamed Boucetta. I called him at a nearby hotel and he graciously agreed to see me and Farah at his hotel, the next day, at 7:00 a.m. Over breakfast, Farah talked to Boucetta and raised the question of the Sahara, of recent developments in the territory, and of the possibility of arriving at a peaceful solution. The

Minister answered his questions with both competence and humility.

Boucetta, at the end, suggested that Farah talk to Driss Slaoui, an advisor

to King Hassan II. I called Driss Slaoui to schedule an appointment with

Farah the following afternoon. His quarters were a well-appointed villa,

not a hotel like for the rest of the summit participants. He received us

with respect but with some degree of coolness. Farah never understood

that coolness, but I did. In the late eighties, when Slaoui had been

Morocco's ambassador to the UN in New York, I had been asked by the

director of the cabinet of UN Secretary-General Perez de Cuéllar to help

him informally on the issue of the Western Sahara where the Polisario

Front, backed by Algeria, had been waging a war against Mauritania and

Morocco. In 1965, the UN General Assembly asked Spain to decolonize

the territory. In 1975, Spain relinquished the administrative control of the

territory to a joint administration by Morocco and Mauritania. A war

erupted between those countries, and the Sahrawi national liberation

movement, the Polisario Front, which proclaimed the Sahrawi Arab

Democratic Republic (SADR) with a government-in-exile in Tindouf,

Algeria. Mauritania withdrew in 1979, and Morocco eventually secured effective control of most of the territory, including all the major cities.

I had done my best at the UN to rebalance the situation regarding the preparations for the referendum in the Sahara from one that was clearly tilted toward the Algerian position. Slaoui had never had a clear idea of what was going on in the Secretariat regarding the Sahara. Unlike his Moroccan predecessors at the United Nations who sought discussion with me on this important question, his arrogance prevented him from asking advice from a staff member deeply knowledgeable about the issue. His weakness: too much arrogance.

Farah asked Slaoui about the Moroccan position on the Western Sahara. I translated both Farah's questions as well as Slaoui's answers. It was a good exchange, but not as warm as the one Farah had held with Boucetta.

The main topic of the Arab Summit of 1982 was to call for the creation of an independent Palestinian state. The Summit recognized the Palestine Liberation Organization (PLO) as the sole legitimate representative of the Palestinian people, and affirmed the right of all the states in the region to live in peace, thus also implicitly recognizing Israel.

Before the UN delegation left Fes to return to New York, I saw Foreign Minister Boucetta again. I suggested that Farah and Kittani be given the opportunity to take a visit to the enchanting city of Marrakech. Boucetta warmly accepted the suggestion, and we were driven in limousines through the beautiful mountains of the Middle Atlas, accompanied by that same official member of the Foreign Ministry who helped get me into the conference at the Royal Palace. Farah and Kittani enjoyed the scenery, even though the trip was a long one. I also arranged for them to visit my native village, Zaouia-Cheikh, midway between Fes and Marrakech.

We arrived there at lunch time. My parents greeted the guests, who responded with a warm embrace. Lunch was already awaiting us: freshly baked whole wheat bread, pancakes, lamb brochettes, and, for dessert, an assortment of fruits and cookies. We rested for about half an hour, drank mint tea, said good-bye to my family, and resumed our trip.

We arrived in Marrakech in mid afternoon, and took rooms in the famous Al Mamounia Hotel with its outside gardens, swimming pool, and mosaic walls. We stayed there two nights. The UN guests thoroughly enjoyed the fabled Jamaâ Lafna square, with its snake charmers, traditional doctors, and enchanting music. They also enjoyed the dinner

at Al Mamounia. Farah loved to start his meal with *harira*, a spicy

vegetable soup containing lentils. He learnt the art of taking in a full

spoon of soup together with a sweet pitted majhool date. For years,

Farah and Kittani would remind me of the wonderful hospitality of

Moroccans.

Two days after arriving to Marrakech, we flew from this city to

Casablanca, then off to New York, to resume our ordinary lives at UN

Headquarters.

The Mystery of Qatar

In 1972, I was the chief of the Sea and Ocean Affairs Section in the

Secretariat, which provided services to the so-called Seabed Committee. I

was involved in all the discussions on the issues related to this subject,

from 1968 to 1974, when the Law of the Sea Conference was inaugurated

in Caracas, Venezuela. For years, we had been working in New York on

the very important issue of oceans: the laws on oceans, straits, fisheries,

scientific research, minerals in the seas and oceans, and the pollution of

this vast oceanic environment. In 1972, the Qatar Government invited

the Seabed Committee to meet in Doha, the capital. Diplomats, UN

Secretariat members, and observers were to meet there to discuss diplomatic negotiations on the complex issues of the oceans. When we landed, Qatari officials were there to welcome us. After taking refreshments—orange juice and pastries—we handed over our passports and got into official limousines. Each member of the United Nations delegation had his or her own limousine. I got into my car, alone. The driver was seated at the wheel, three rows in front of me. When I greeted him, he responded with a smile.

Even forty years ago, the Doha Hotel was modern. Colorful teletype machines lined the lobby. Outside, the blue ocean was bordered by the golden beach. I asked someone how they could, in the desert strip separating the airport from the hotel, maintain a row of green trees, flower beds, and green grass. I was told that they went to Latin America in search for plants, bushes, and trees that resisted heat and drought, and brought them to Qatar. They were very expensive.

We were taken to large rooms with beautiful views, before gathering in the restaurant for a sumptuous meal. We ate Las Vegas style from an abundant buffet. Talk about Arab generosity! We each filled up our large plates, sat down on comfortable chairs, and began to savor our appetizing food. For drinks, we were served every type of mineral water, as well as fruits and tropical juices, all imported from outside. Some diplomats searched for a glass or bottle of wine or beer. There were none. They were told that the king came to pray in the hotel, so it held no public display of wine or spirits.

Since work had not started, Ambassador Hamilton Shirley Amerasinghe of Sri Lanka, the president of the Committee, approached me. "Abbadi," he said, "please find out where we can have a drink anywhere in this hotel!"

"Yes, Mr. President," I answered, "I will." I headed toward the reception desk, where I tried to explain that diplomats are accustomed to having drinks. I told the clerk that the UN delegation was looking for a place to do just that, and asked him where they could go for that purpose. He murmured quietly a few words, and resumed his work at his counter. I understood there was no place in the hotel to have a drink. So, a moment after, I went to see Ambassador Amerasinghe, and relayed what I thought was a negative answer.

Later that evening, the Ambassador saw me again, and he again made the same request. He added that several diplomats were equally looking forward to a drink. "Go see the ambassador of Qatar," Amerasinghe said to me. I then went to speak to the Qatar ambassador to the United Nations about the matter, who directed me to the same reception desk. When I relayed once more the message to the receptionist with the addition of the Qatar ambassador's name, he said in a very low voice: "Go to room 402." Clearly, he did not wish to be overheard.

When I told Ambassador Amerasinghe of the answer—"room 402"—he was glad to hear it. He shared this information with colleagues, and together they would visit room 402 to have a drink.

By this time it was nearly seven in the evening. An impatient delegate went to 402 on the fourth floor and rang the bell. As he relayed the story later on, a tall blond woman in her pink silk gown opened the door. The diplomat simply walked in. The woman, astonished, asked him what he wanted. "To have a drink," he hurriedly said. The woman, smiling, informed him there was no bar there. The receptionist had given me the wrong number! Delegates in need of a drink could go to room 502. I so informed Ambassador Amerasinghe later that night. He immediately took my hand, called on a couple of diplomats who were nearby in the hall, and asked me to lead them to the appropriate room. We took the elevator to the fifth floor.

I started looking for the room, but could not find it. There were no door knobs, no clear demarcation between the door frames. Nevertheless, one of the delegates pushed what looked like a line in a white wall. Suddenly, the door opened. Amerasinghe entered first. I followed him. Beyond that, there seemed to be no door, again. By this time, we learned to just look for a fine, almost invisible, line in the wall. We found one. The Ambassador pushed it. Once more we were in a tiny empty space. Then the Ambassador interjected, "This is like a thousand and one nights; open sesame !" The third push, and finally and suddenly we discovered a small bar. A few people were seated there, having drinks. Our diplomats joined the group. I left them to go help in the preparations for the next day's meeting. The mystery was uncovered. Our diplomats were satisfied. The next day we rolled up our sleeves and began to do our work.

Chapter 13
The United Nations at a Crossroads

The UN is now at a crossroads because its financial resources have diminished, while its mandate has considerably expanded. It is somewhat sidestepped by regional organizations. I see some potential signs of decline, similar to those of its predecessor, the League of Nations.

Long-standing crises include the sixty-five-year-old Israeli-Palestinian conflict. Current crises include: Syria, Libya, the environment, poverty, and terrorism. I postulate that the UN needs not only to reform but also to innovate urgently to avoid the risk of finding itself irrelevant at some point in the future.

Work life at the UN has been a fulfilling experience. I will forever be grateful to the International House at UC Berkeley for preparing me for the global society, but it was the United Nations that gave me the chance to actually experience the truly international experience.

On the other hand, the same fulfilling experience has at the same time led me to conclude that the United Nations, in its present form, has only a limited role to play in an ever-globalizing world. With its modest budget, it cannot be expected to move the world ahead. It cannot deal successfully with every single major conflict. It cannot improve the standard of living of everyone, everywhere. It cannot put an end to poverty. It cannot bring peace to all the countries.

But the United Nations can, and does, make some difference in the lives of some people in some places, sometimes. The real strength of the organization lies not only in the good work that it does to promote peace and security, but in its promotion of the values that keep hope alive for a better world. In this context, the United Nations Charter is our guiding light. Regrettably, it has been violated on a regular basis, and in recent decades, the ideals that led to the establishment of the UN have shifted.

For its first thirty years, through the early seventies, the UN was on the side of the people who fought against oppression, for progress. It was a beacon for people and nations all over the world, especially in the developing countries, the so-called third world.

As the world began to experience economic crises in the late seventies, and UN resources diminished, it began to feel pressures from the major contributing countries. The result was financial retrenchment, a situation that persists today. The financial wings of the organization have been trimmed.

Through the process of reorganization, restructuring, centralization, decentralization, and reduction of permanent contracts, the UN has kept costs down. The policy of change of internal culture, including mobility, has lowered the morale among the staff. The change of culture, which encouraged the presence of personnel from the developing world in the seventies and eighties, began to favor staff from the developed world in the late 1990s and early 2000s. This has led to a reduction in cultural diversity in the organization. The policy of mobility that made room for these staff members at the UN headquarters has also led to decline in staff morale.

Still, the United Nations has initiated reforms under the administrations of various secretaries-general, but these reforms have not always been innovative. Instead, some have led to unexpected outcomes: the discouragement of the well-qualified international staff. This professional staff was put on short leashes, via limited term contracts. Thus, they felt uncertain as to their future in the organization, the renewal of their contracts, and their chances of promotion. Some of them began to seek the help of permanent missions to reach their personal career objectives. This, in turn, has led to a politicized situation, to the present state of discouragement, decline in staff morale, and, more importantly, to a reduction in the quality of staff work.

The ideals that inspired the first thirty years of the United Nations were no longer the guiding lights. New colleagues ignored what the Charter mandates. Discussions among staff members in the cafeteria were no longer about the ideas and ideals of international cooperation, but about gossip of who was seen with whom at parties and meetings. The United Nations seems to be undergoing a change of voice from the professional to the personal. Years ago, the speeches of the secretary-general were characterized by an international, collective quality, such as "we," "the United Nations," or "the international organization." Today, that language has been replaced by that of the "I" and the "me." The question that arises naturally, at this stage in my mind, is what to do now. I do not pretend to have the answer(s), but I do have some suggestions.

Clearly, the United Nations is no longer well equipped financially, or intellectually, to deal effectively with all the world's major problems. At the present stage, nations do not seem prepared for the burden of additional significant financial contributions. This situation arises at a time when the UN has been given a multiplicity of additional new responsibilities. It has spread its wings too much, and therefore, the time has come for a serious review of its agenda. I wish, in the following, to suggest some significant changes.

The organization should shed some of its numerous peripheral issues and activities, in the same way as many private enterprises have done. It should concentrate on a limited number of core issues: peace and security, disarmament, economic development, cooperation, poverty, human rights, the environment. It can leave many other activities to its constituencies, member states, or specialized agencies, which can deal with these matters more efficiently.

The United Nations should, in accordance with the provision of its charter in Article 109, hold a General Conference to review and amend the present charter. A number of departments should be eliminated and reduced to general divisions with a minimum of five general areas within each division. The post of under-secretary-general should be eliminated and replaced by a senior executive director at the D-3 level. In the UN, the letter P stands for professional, D, for Director, the last stage of the professional class. The international chief executive would replace the current secretary-general. The senior executive directors will form the Executive Council of the international chief executive.

All special envoys, personal envoys, special representatives, and personal representatives whose posts have proliferated during the last decades should be eliminated. Instead, a regional executive representative should be appointed for each of the five major regions in the world. Together with a core staff, the regional executive representative would be located in the capital of each of the regions, near the center of crises and developments. The present Department of Public Information (DPI) should be sharply restructured. Its mandate and functions should be reformulated and subcontracted to a global communication firm, responsible to the international chief executive and staffed with personnel from all five continents. The Department of Public Information is supposed to project the image of the United Nations throughout the world, by bringing to the people all the information available on the work of the organization. Yet, this department has clearly not been successful in its important mission.

Sure, the defenders of the department will rush to point to the polls conducted in the United States about the work of the United Nations, showing that 64 percent of the American people endorse the work of the international organization. However, the results of those polls do not reveal the entire situation. First, they do depend on the nature of the question asked, and the audience to which it is addressed. In this case, I suspect the question was something like this: Do you support the UN work? It was not asked this way: Where does UN work stand as a priority? The answer would have been altogether different. Second, I further suspect that the question was addressed to a community of highly educated people, intellectuals, academics, and members of private foundations.

The fact is that when you travel around the world as many of us have done, you hear people talk negatively about the United Nations. They list all kinds of arguments, ranging from the United Nations waging wars against small countries and practicing double standards, to being incapable of resolving major crises and conflicts such as genocide in Rwanda, the Palestinian-Israeli conflict, Syrian conflict, or climate change and poverty. Why are many people feeling this way about the United

Nations? In a major way, that is due, to a large extent, to the failure of DPI to project the true UN image to the world. There are many reasons behind this shortcoming. I will cite only some of the important ones.

DPI continues to use uninspiring, bureaucratic, and old ways of informing world public opinion about the work of the organization. The story of DPI has been told since the sixties, especially by the head of this department in his now forgotten book, *The Play within the Play, The Inside Story of the United Nations*. (8) DPI relies on the issuance of communiqués and reports written in an incomprehensible language which many do not read. It further relies on the multiplicity of UN Centers in various capitals in the world, who receive UN documents with considerable delay, and this, in the age of the Internet. It also relies on its publication, the *Monthly Chronicle*, lacking depth and analysis. Its radio and television programs are characterized by boredom and a lack of excitement.

There are, however, active organizations and groups that try to inform world public opinion and that do a reasonably good work. They include the United Nations Association-USA (UNA-USA) and CTAUN (Committee on the Teaching about the United Nations). I sit on the

Advisory Council of CTAUN. The latter is a group of dedicated women working enthusiastically to inform the public through conferences and workshops. They are always busy like bees pollinating flowers except in their case they pollinate the minds of young people through their educators. (9)

Clearly, DPI can inform public opinion in a more creative way, using modern means of management and communication. The true story about the United Nations, of peace and humanity, remains to be told more effectively. I suggest that DPI become an office, and that it engage in a partnership with a private modern global communication company to project that message in a better way.

In the first place, DPI is limited in what it can say, as well as in the availability of information it has at its disposal. The United Nations is not known for its transparency, despite the secretary-general's repetition to the contrary. In a letter I sent to Kofi Annan, I suggested some ways in which he could open further the glass house. (10)

Moreover, the Security Council, in particular, as seen previously, holds by far more private consultations than open meetings. The public has no knowledge about what is being discussed behind closed doors.

Even delegates, nonmembers of the Security Council, are not privy to those meetings. One learns more about them at cocktail receptions. Sure, the president of the Council from time to time informs other members about the content of the consultations, but this effort remains limited.

Another problem resides in the fact that the secretary-general is reluctant to exercise his prerogatives under Article 99 of the Charter, which empowers him to bring to the attention of the Council any matter which in his view might threaten international peace and security. To achieve this goal, the United Nations needs a strong international leader. But the great powers do not want such a leadership. The UN therefore faces a conundrum. Only public and international pressure would one day change this situation.

Crucial to its work and to its future, the United Nations should begin to gradually transfer work to regional organizations, such as the African Union, European Union, Organization of American States, Association of Southeast Asian Nations (ASEAN), and the League of Arab States. Assistance to individual states or sub regions should gradually become the combined work of the UN regional representative and the executive director of each region. The United Nations should help the regional states achieve a process of regional integration. This is crucial to lessening interstate and intrastate conflicts, and to reducing bilateral tension and wars. Regional integration is the future. The United Nations should be in the front, the leading engine for change, not the red lantern at the back of the old train.

Even more important, the United Nations must, from this point on, take as its first priority the establishment of an Integrated Conflict Resolution Center (ICRC), with preventive diplomacy and a Crisis Alert System (CAS) as its core. The organization has spent much effort, too many resources and too much time in cleaning up after conflicts. Prevention should be the priority goal. Diplomacy, negotiation, arbitration, and conciliation should be its means.

Those means are provided for in the UN Charter, but they are not consistently utilized in addressing root causes of tensions and conflicts. That is partly because preventive diplomacy is not viewed by the UN as a priority. How else could one explain the meager resources devoted to this field? As seen before, the budget for peacekeeping represents an enormous sum, on the order of eight billion dollars. The budget for preventive diplomacy amounts to a pathetic biennium sum of 1.2 million

191

dollars for the Department of Political Affairs. Preventive diplomacy, which anticipates problems and nips them in the bud in general, takes a lower profile than peacekeeping, the expensive correction of problems that have grown out of control.

The ICRC should have as its head a senior executive director at the D-3 level and constitute a unit distinct from the general divisions. It should be staffed with personnel with special competence in the political field, including diplomatic skills in negotiation, conciliation, and strategic research and analysis. The Center should work in close cooperation with the international chief executive and with the members of the Security Council.

The General Assembly should innovate in such a way as to include five representatives from the civil society, one from each of the five continents. They should enjoy the right to vote. Regarding peacekeeping, the United Nations should not involve itself in every internal conflict in the world. It should limit itself to intervening in serious cases that are likely to lead to massive human rights violations and genocide. The UN should avoid intervening in all cases of internal civil wars. It should not be seen, as some see it today, as an organization "waging wars against people." The budget of peacekeeping should be reduced by half from its present eight billion dollars.

The international chief executive should be elected for one single term of six years. His travel budget, which amounts to more than two million dollars today, should be cut to half that amount. Modern communication technology should allow the international chief executive to conduct business with the outside world from his headquarters in New York.

Additionally, in a move of affirmative action, the international chief executive should submit four names of female candidates from four geographical regions to the General Assembly, for the post of deputy international chief executive. No such candidate can come from the region of the international chief executive.

The Security Council, instead of simply resorting to statements condemning one party or another, should sit in its unofficial meetings as an active party to negotiations. It should regularly invite the parties to the conflict, hear their side, and, with the assistance of the ICRC, formulate suggestions and alternatives for defusing tension, heading off a crisis, and finding a long term solution to the situation. In recent decades, the Security Council has been too passive, relying on verbal or written pronouncements that are not practical in the search for solutions. Its statements have been inflationary and ineffective.

I am aware that my ideas are bold. Some of them may be seen as an attempt to turn the United Nations into a private entity. I have no such desire. In fact, I am seeking the opposite aim: to establish an independent institution that serves all citizens of the world. It should be obvious that some UN members would not want to see in the secretary-general a chief executive. That is my point. At the present time, the secretary-general is a mere figurehead, with no real power. The time has come for an Executive, a true leader of the organization, a Dag Hammarskjöld type, with courage, passion, and vision. The twenty-first century requires that.

Chapter 14
Inching toward a Global Society

The twentieth century was distinguished by the devastation of two world wars, oppression of minorities, local conflicts, and terrorism. But at the same time, it was a time of liberation for millions of people trapped in colonialism and apartheid. Even though extreme Islamic terrorists attacked the World Trade Center and the Pentagon in the United States, the Roman Pope John Paul II, leader of more than a billion Catholics, was announcing that humanity, with its wisdom and virtue, was actually entering into the new century with great promises. He affirmed that with these gifts, with the help of God's grace, we can build in the next century a civilization worthy of the human person, a true culture of freedom. (11) While some of us have witnessed the transition from a traditional society to an open one, our grandchildren will witness the advent of yet another new epoch: the Global Society.

I believe that the road to the Global Society will be long and tortuous. Humanity will evolve through various stages before it stabilizes in the midst of this great mosaic of civilized nations. Clearly, the forces of globalization and interdependence are at work even today, gradually transforming the various independent entities into vast networks of connected world communities. Trade, the Internet, tourism, and international telecommunications bring regions together in a new Age of Discovery.

The first step toward the Global Society will be regional integration in each continent. At the present time, the trends toward regional integration are to be found in the ever increasing incapacity of individual countries to face the stiff competition of larger ones, or of groups of countries, in the rising search for more extended market space and the inefficiency of small ones, and in the search for comparative advantages arising from economies of large scale. Regional integration in a continent can be given life by a sub-regional integration as we are witnessing in North, East, and West Africa. Regional integration is underway in Latin America and Asia. Europe has already formed a Union, which continues to strengthen and expand.

In addition to regional integration, the conclusion of free trade agreements between states or regions, including the recent Transpacific and Transatlantic Partnership, is accelerating the process of world globalization.

The second stage toward a Global Society will be the establishment of a Global Partnership. The Breton Woods institutions of the post–World War II era, and the World Bank and the International Monetary Fund of the postwar period, like the United Nations, must undergo great transformations. These institutions will prove to be inadequate in the times of regional integration. Each continent would establish its own regional bank, and the world would one day need to create a Central Global Bank, a sort like the Federal Reserve Bank in Washington, DC.

At the political level, the Security Council should expand and reconfigure. Germany, Japan, India, South Africa, Nigeria, Brazil, or Mexico, and maybe an Arab country, should gain a permanent seat on the Security Council with or without the right of the veto. The Council would be small, with a membership of just over twenty, with an agenda reflecting priority issues. Regional representation would give the Security Council a more representative character than it has presently.

Humanity will continue to progress toward higher stages. Transformative changes will occur in all fields, in science and technology, including the environment, biology, space, and the oceans. Education will emphasize global aspects, including world geography, history, culture, and civilizations.

One of the most transformative changes that will take place would be in the field of humanities, especially our value system. Compassion, human solidarity, and the interdependence of hearts will lead to the humanization of regional and global relations. Assistance to children, elderly, and the underprivileged will take on new dimensions. Poverty will become increasingly morally unacceptable. Help in natural disaster crises will become a moral responsibility and will attract a greater number of volunteers, especially among youth.

In the era of Global Society, a rich, diversified, and advanced civilization will develop gradually. It will be a synthesis of all major civilizations, old and new. There will be no dominant civilization in the age of Global Society. The new planetary civilization will manifest many advances in science, art, music, and the humanities. It will be characterized by not just common humanity, but also by advanced thinking. For the first time in human history, the Global Society will not hold that war is inevitable. It may actually ban the institution of war. The Global Society will witness the increasing moralization of global relations.

Spiritual leaders will play an important role. Spirituality will be the shining light in the culture of the new world mosaic civilization.

My former professor, Leslie Lipson, writes, "What humanity most needs in the twenty-first century is a new axial age: a revolution in ethical consciousness as profound as those that occurred simultaneously in several civilizations during the period from the seventh to the fifth century BC, and later in the Western civilization during the Enlightenment of the eighteenth century and the Age of Progress in the nineteenth." (12)

Professor Lipson added that "if the twenty-first century should be fortunate enough to generate a third Axial Age, its philosophy should be akin to that of the second-secular, rationalist, and humanist. Its intellectual foundations must be rooted in science, in the findings of research into humanity's past, in the exercise of critical intelligence, in the weighing of evidence and drawing of judgments from empirical data." (13)

How do we arrive at a Global Society where better ethical values are established? The spiritualist Nicolya Christi has one vision of how this will happen. "A new epoch founded upon a new consciousness that holds at its core a visionary new global system is dependent entirely upon the fearless who are willing to blaze a trail and light the way for the establishment of a new global culture—one that fulfills its primary role to nurture the well-being of the individual and the collective and, by so doing, manifest sustainable world peace." (14)

Scientific discoveries raise the question of their limits and their implications. Humankind will then begin to search for ways to temper its relentless pursuit of material accumulation. The twenty-first century will be marked by humankind's renewed search for ways of satisfying its nonmaterial needs. It will be the century of spiritual renewal, synthesis of human values, and journey to oneness. Men and women will begin to experience the joy of their common humanity, of the liberation of their human spirit, and the fulfillment of their human dignity.

Humanity will continue to ascend toward more advanced stages, in a long spiritual journey, to discover human links to the cosmic world, and our place in this vast universe. We will embark on a spiritual journey to a higher consciousness, which will help us acquire the global spirit and the consciousness to tackle together the multiplicity of global issues facing humankind.

In the meantime, the global community will progress toward the mosaic civilization, characterized by giant technological realizations, by a great human diversity, and by global human interconnectedness. Bridges and tunnels will be built between united and integrated continents. Europe and Africa, for example, will be linked by an undersea tunnel or a bridge between Spain and Morocco. At the present, Chinese engineers are said to be in talks over the construction of a high-speed railway spanning from the northeast coast of China to the United States, via Siberia and the Bering Strait. Other railway projects under discussion would link China to Southeast and Central Asia, and to other destinations like London and Tehran. One railroad that would run to Turkey is intended to retrace the steps of the ancient Silk Road.

With the beginning of the mosaic civilization, people from every continent will be on the move, crossing borders and seeking cultural enjoyments. They will travel to outer space and to inner space (the oceans) and visit laboratories, undersea museums, and gardens. They will stay at houses built under the oceans and land and take off from airport platforms on the surface of the seas and oceans. People needing rest and quietness will find them in sanatoriums in the depths of the silent oceans.

We will celebrate science fiction set in the future, like *Two Thousand Leagues under the Sea*, as well as those histories about the ancient Silk Road.

Five hundred million Chinese will travel the world's roads and so will fifty million Africans. This vast movement will transform the face of our planet. Mandarin will be widely spoken; races will mix like never before. The cultures, the arts, and music will attain a high degree of enrichment and diversity.

In the vast development of the mosaic civilization, the human spirit is bound to expand and enlarge. As Dag Hammarskjöld pointed out, "Peace begins in our private worlds."

Humankind will, like a giant family, feel the bonds that unite its diverse members to each other, and beyond that, to its environment, that is, to the vast universe. As Albert Einstein pointed out, widening our horizons and observing the world around us will be key. "Our task," he said, "must be to free ourselves from this prison by widening our circle of compassion to embrace all living creatures and the whole of nature in its beauty." (15)

In the age of the global society, the spiritual leaders, the Pope, Buddhist Master, Rabbi, Imam, and others representing the earth's 33,000 religious leaders, will play an increasingly important role. The global community will celebrate together all the major spiritual holidays, such as the Day of Vesac, which marks the birth, enlightenment and passing of Buddha.

Speaking on that occasion on May 13, 2014, Secretary-General Ban Ki-moon declared that "the teachings of peace, compassion, and love can inspire our efforts to address many of the broader challenges confronting our world: peace, security, development, and the protection of the environment." He further said, "In each of these areas, we have to rise above narrow self-interest, and think and act as members of one global community." (16)

Chapter 15
Born in the Gardens Again

The author's granddaughter, Yasmina, enchanted by the garden.

This book reflects my personal story, my long journey from the cave to the global society of the twenty-first century, whose contours are still emerging. I began the story in the midst of the gardens of my native village of Zaouia-Cheikh. I will end it under the big aok tree next to my gardens in the Berkshires, on the New York/Massachusetts border.

My experience in the United States and at the university taught me some of the most important values of the American people. My half-century professional life under the roof of the United Nations gave me the opportunity to live the life of a global citizen and to be conscious of the interconnectedness of all nations and peoples.

Beyond that, retreats in my gardens have led me to be mindful, through further contemplation and meditation, of the harmony in the universe and of the links of all living creatures to a higher force.

The author under the big oak tree in his garden.

The Breezy Hill Gardens is the quiet and inspiring natural site where I have retreated on weekends for some thirty years now. There, together with the help of my wife and my children when they were young, I cultivated the land and maintained a small orchard of various fruit trees. I also gave a hand to my wife in caring for her flower beds and herb garden. It is par excellence a place that offers me, just like when I was young, the opportunity of contemplation and meditation in the midst of the majesty and mystery of nature.

For thirty years, I have observed nature in the midst of its renewal and creation. Everything in nature reveals its many miraculous aspects: the smell of freshly plowed ground or of cut grass, the blooming of apple trees, the songs of birds, the slow activity of bumblebees working on the pollination of flowers, and the shadow of a baby deer standing on the porch. Nature offers us many lessons: the changes in seasons, like the changes in the state of the human condition; the patience of seeing a tiny seed turn into a seven-foot plant; the orderly and harmonious activities of all living creatures, humans and animals; the changes in weather, rain, and sun; the diversity of the world; and the fragility of mother earth.

The perception of this miracle is accentuated on a clear night when you look at the sky and see the face of the moon illuminating the pond of the neighbors and the eyes of the baby rabbit standing still in the grass.

But beyond the visible world, like the early rise of the sun or the scintillating stars at night, there is the invisible, the silent, the deep, and the spaceless world. One can only feel it. Contemplation and meditation make one conscious of it. It is a much larger world, an immense one. It is the universe.

To feel a really full life, one must, through one's imagination, transcend the borders of our world and of one's cultural conditioning. Beyond the beauty and generosity of nature, there is the beauty and love of the divine, about whom Jalal Uddin Rumi was so passionate. The Sufis tell us that there are two ways of transcending our world. One way is to look at the universe and see ourselves. The other way is to look within ourselves and see the universe.

Chapter 16
New Spirituality

In the age of the global society, spirituality goes beyond meditation, love, and compassion. It involves a greater degree of open-mindedness. It also concerns a deep commitment to the large goal of the betterment of the human condition.

Looking forward, I believe that the highest leaders of the major faiths—Christianity, Judaism, Islam, Buddhism, and Hinduism—will one day want to form an interfaith council to recommend specific measures to tackle the burning questions facing the human race. This responsibility should be shared by all those who feel that the spiritual community cannot stay indifferent in the age of the global society. This does not mean that I recommend that the spiritual community involve itself in the political domain but rather simply encourage its members to take the moral responsibility to engage more in social actions. (17)

We already see that the premium American society places on money is somewhat fading. Material accumulation is now considered, by some, more of a superficial endeavor, while most young people are putting effort into the intellectual, spiritual, and cultural emancipation of the individual person in society. Nations in the world will compete less in the field of economics or armaments but more in the area of culture, including music, the arts, and sports.

In the age of the global society, emphasis will be placed on the quality of the human condition, including the satisfaction of the spiritual and social needs of the individuals in the community. Basic needs such as clean and safe water, food, good health, housing, and a clean environment will become part of a person's larger human rights.

People in the global society will feel more interconnected than ever before. Professional associations such as those of educators, lawyers, journalists, and other groups of the civil society will form global organizations "without borders" and will meet regularly in different countries and continents. Their members will acquire new skills in various languages and a new awareness of the diversity of cultures.

In the global society, a new spirituality will develop with the birth of an unprecedented consciousness: the mindfulness of the needs of others. This mindfulness will be cultivated to a full realization that we are only a small part of the global community and the universe, that our present and our future as human beings are inextricably interconnected, and that each one of us has a role and an obligation to fulfill in building the foundations of a peaceful world.

"If civilization is to survive," observed Franklin D. Roosevelt, "we must cultivate the science of human relationships—the ability of all peoples, of all kinds, to live together, in the same world at peace."

The author receiving a royal decoration from His Highness Prince Moulay Rachid of Morocco.

The author giving a conference at the University Sultan Moulay Slimane, Beni-Mellal, Morocco, March 2013.

Appendix

Letter to Secretary-General Kofi Annan

PERSONNEL ET CONFIDENTIEL

Le 5 mars 1997

Monsieur le Secrétaire général,

J'ai l'honneur de vous faire parvenir la lettre ci-jointe qui traite brièvement de la situation intérieure au sein du Secrétariat, et à travers laquelle je formule quelques suggestions, en espérant qu'elles contribueront à améliorer la situation interne. Je me tiens à votre disposition pour avancer d'autres recommandations, en détail, à cet effet.

Comme vous pourrez le constater, la lettre que je vous adresse aujourd'hui est écrite sous la forme d'un article susceptible d'être publié. Je vous serais donc très reconnaissant de bien vouloir me faire connaître votre avis sur le sujet. Voyez-vous un inconvénient à ce que la lettre soit publiée ?

Veuillez agréer, Monsieur le Secrétaire général, l'expression de ma très haute considération, et de mes sentiments les meilleurs.

Abdelkader Abbadi,
Ancien Directeur de la
Division Afrique II,
Département des Affaires politiques

Les Nations Unies
Lettre au Secrétaire général

Abdelkader ABBADI*

Mon frère Kofi, comme nous disons dans notre culture africaine,

comme toi, j'ai passé une trentaine d'années au Secrétariat des Nations Unies. Tu étais quelquefois assis en face de moi, dans la salle de conférences adjacente à ton bureau, et ensemble avec nos collègues nous discutions des crises en Angola, au Mozambique, au Rwanda, au Zaïre... Et j'ai toujours apprécié ta sérénité, tes connaissances profondes, ta modération et ta franchise. Pourquoi je t'envoie cette lettre ? C'est d'abord par conviction, et ensuite parce que tu es engagé dans les réformes et que tu as ouvertement opté pour la transparence. Tu m'excuseras donc si je dois toucher dans cette lettre de choses que tu connais bien. Et, en disant ce que je vais dire, ce n'est en aucun cas pour critiquer l'Organisation ou entacher son image. J'ai passé toute ma carrière au service de cette Organisation. Je crois en son avenir et en sa renaissance. Et, si les Nations Unies n'étaient pas là, il faudrait les créer.

Mon frère Kofi, pendant quatre décennies, comme tu le sais, les Nations Unies ont connu des temps glorieux. On y allait travailler, non pas pour gagner de l'argent et devenir riche, mais pour participer à la réalisation de ses nobles idéaux, pour partager un peu son prestige qui rayonnait dans le monde, et pour faire partie de ce corps spécial de fonctionnaires internationaux dévoués et engagés, recrutés dans les quatre coins du monde pour leurs connaissances, leurs hautes qualités, leur intégrité et leur indépendance. Ils faisaient esprit de corps dans leurs efforts enthousiastes et leurs élans destinés à contribuer à renforcer la paix et la sécurité internationales, à aider les peuples colonisés à s'affranchir et à se développer. Parmi les noms les plus prestigieux, toi et moi, mon frère, nous avons connu des hommes comme Ralph Bunche et Andrew Cordier (Etats-Unis), Omar Loutfi (Egypte), Brian Urquhart (Royaume-Uni), Constantin Stavropoulos (Grèce), Kenneth Dadzie (Ghana), Philippe de Seynes (France), F.T. Liu (China), George Sherry (Etats-Unis), et j'en passe. Par leur savoir, leur culture, leur tact et leur humilité, ces grands hommes étaient inspirés et ils inspiraient, à leur tour, leurs collègues au Secrétariat et les diplomates dans les salles de conférences. On s'enorgueillait à dire aux gens en dehors de l'enceinte des Nations Unies que l'on travaillait pour l'Organisation internationale, et on était reçu avec la plus grande déférence par le grand public. Les troupes des Nations Unies se voyaient octroyer le Prix Nobel pour leur courage et leur efficacité dans leurs missions difficiles de maintien de la paix. Le prestige de l'Organisation était à son comble.

Tout cela a bien changé ces dernières années, mon frère !

Dans leurs missions, les soldats onusiens sont quelquefois tués, mal menés, ou faits prisonniers. Au Secrétariat, personne ne peut nier le fait qu'il s'est établi, au fil des années, une atmosphère de doute et de cynisme. Tu connais, mon frère, les principaux facteurs qui ont mené à cette situation. La qualité du travail s'est détériorée, résultat d'une politique de recrutement et de promotion partisane, qui a mené au remplacement de l'excellence par le culte de la médiocrité, de l'engagement par le découragement, du dévouement par les calculs à court terme. La gestion transparente et décentralisée a cédé la place à une gestion centralisée, secrète, caractérisée par le favoritisme, l'établissement de grands fiefs au Secrétariat, animés par des barons qui se spécialisent dans l'échange et la négoce des postes, et par des groupes de pression. Ils ont tous oublié le sermon qu'ils ont fait lors de la prise de leurs fonctions : qu'ils étaient au service de la communauté internationale.

Il y a aussi, mon frère, la politisation des postes au Secrétariat, l'intervention extérieure, et ces facteurs combinés à d'autres ont contribué à affaiblir la fonction internationale. Il est certain qu'un fonctionnaire international neutre ne peut aujourd'hui facilement coexister avec le fonctionnaire soutenu politiquement. C'est la coexistence entre le pot de fer et le pot de terre. Dans la compétition, ce dernier n'allait pas loin, ou ne survivait pas. Le corps des fonctionnaires est divisé et tiraillé.

Aujourd'hui, mon frère, le Secrétariat subit le contrecoup d'une crise financière. Mais, plus grave encore, c'est la crise morale qui sévit en son sein. Il est plus facile, à mon avis, d'obtenir les fonds qui font défaut depuis plusieurs années que de résusciter et de réhabiliter des âmes découragées. Certes, il se trouve encore dans le Secrétariat des fonctionnaires de grande culture, de grande expérience et dont l'intégrité n'a jamais été entamée par ce qu'ils ont vu se passer autour d'eux ces dernières années, mais certains subissent le sort de l'exil interne, ou ont déjà quitté l'Organisation qu'ils ont servie avec tant de dévouement, pour d'autres fonctions.

Mon frère, la question qui doit surgir dans ton esprit, j'en suis sûr, c'est comment sortir de cette situation ? Comment l'assainir et rétablir la confiance, l'efficacité, le dévouement aux principes et objectifs de l'Organisation ? Voilà un des défis qu'on t'a lancé. Tu sais, come doivent le savoir les gouvernements, qu'aucune réforme ne pourrait être couronnée de succès si elle ne tenait pas compte de l'état d'âme de cette armée de fonctionnaires un peu désarmée à l'heure actuelle, critiquée, incomprise, blessée par tant d'années de négligence, d'indifférence de la part de ceux qui, au cours des années, refusaient d'admettre que des problèmes existaient et demeuraient sans solution.

La médiocrité sera difficile à vaincre, car elle est structurellement bien établie. Mais la situation est loin d'être fatale. Elle nécessite des réformes urgentes et en profondeur. Comme la nomination d'un Groupe d'Experts nationaux qui sera chargé du recrutement du personnel (les temps sont venus pour soustraire ce domaine aux mains des barons); l'établissement d'un Groupe de spécialistes indépendants chargé de mettre franchement et sérieusement en oeuvre la diplomatie préventive, moins coûteuse qu'une politique de déploiement de forces, et qui

cessite un travail à long terme, d'analyse et de réflexion; une plus grande
verture des Nations Unies au grand public, à travers, par example, une réunion
nuelle au siège pour les penseurs des cinq continents (Prix Nobel de la Paix);
le lancement d'une télévision, d'une radio et d'une revue indépendantes et
ofessionnelles des Nations Unies, pour informer le monde des objectifs, des
tivités et des réalisation de l'Organisation.

Mon frère Kofi, à l'entrée du Secrétariat, côté Nord, se trouve cette
ande sphère en bronze offerte aux Nations Unies par le gouvernement italien et
artiste italien célèbre - Arnaldo Pomodoro. Elle est fracturée, et à
intérieur, elle contient une autre sphère. Le monde semble fracturé, les
tions Unies aussi, mais la sphère interieure représente un monde nouveau qui
t en train de naître. Les Nations Unies représentent l'espoir des peuples pour
paix. Pour ne pas les décevoir, l'Organisation doit faire face aux défis du
Ie siècle. Elle a besoin d'un esprit nouveau, de nouvelles énergies, et d'une
uvelle vision. Tu as la chance historique de contribuer à ce renouveau. Je
souhaite bonne chance, et bon courage.

* Le docteur Abbadi, Marocain,
  était jusqu'au 31 janvier 1997
  Directeur au Département des
  Affaires politiques aux
  Nations Unies

The big Bronze Sphere offered to the United Nations by the Italian Government and the famous Italian Artist Arnaldo Pomodoro, showing a a fractured world and a new emerging world.

Bibliography

1. Javier Péres de Cuéllar, *Pilgrimage for Peace, 1997,* New York: Saint Martin Press, 175 Fifth Avenue, New York, NY, 10010. 358. ..

2. Boutros Boutros-Ghali, *Report on the Work of the Organization* (September 1992): 6, 14.

3. "Syria Crisis: Kofi Annan Resigns as Peace Envoy," www.theguardian.com/world/middle-east-live/2012/aug02/Syria-crisis-Damascus-measures-live-#block-50loaf3195cb5feda7f95881.

4. Abdelkader Abbadi, "Council Big Powers Unlikely to Yield Hard-Won Veto Prerogative," *UN Observer and International Report* (March 1998).

5. Abdelkader Abbadi, *Vision for a New Civilization:* Spiritual and Ethical Values in the New Millennium, August 2000, Won Buddhism Publishing, New York.

6. Nicolya Christi, *Contemporary Spirituality for an Evolving World,* (Toronto: Bear & Company, One Park Street, Rochester, Vermont, 05767, 2013), 219.

7. Pope Francis, *The Joy of the Gospel, the World* among Us Press, Frederick, Maryland, 2013, page 166-167.

8. Hernane Tavares de Sà, *The Play Within the Play*, New York, Alfred A. Knopf, 1966.

9. CTAUN stands for The Committee on the Teaching about the United Nations.

10. Abdelkader Abbadi, Letter to Secretary-General Kofi Annan, dated 5 March, 1997, unpublished, see Annex.

11. Pope Paul John II, "Address to the General Assembly of the United Nations," October 5, 1995.

12. Leslie Lipson, *The Ethical Crises of Civilizations*, Newbury Park, California. Sage Publications, 1993, 299

13. Ibid., 299.

14. Christi, 225.

15. Alice Calaprice, "Dear Professor Einstein," Albert Einstein to and from children, Princeton University Press, 2002.

16. *UN Daily News*, May 13, 2014. a daily document reflecting the most important developments covered by the United Nations.

17. Abdelkader Abbadi, Vision for a New Civilization, Won Visionary Activists, Changing Humanity one Breath at a Time, VHS (New York: Won Buddhism UN & International Office, 2013).

Further Reading

F. Y. Chi, *Consultation and Consensus in the Security Council: A UNITAR Study* (New York: *UNITAR*, 1971).

James O. C. Jonah, *What Price the Survival of the United Nations? Memoirs of a Veteran International Civil Servant* (Nigeria: Evans Bros., 2006),

Tommy Koh, *The Quest for World Order* (Singapore: Institute of Policy Studies, 1998),

Lansana Kouyaté, *Du Brazier Somalien à La Chaleur Onusiènne*, Editions Panthéon, Paris, 2014.)

Jean Richardot, *Journey for a Better World: A Personal Adventure in War and Peace, An Inside Story of the U.N.* (University Press of America, Lanham, 1993).

Stephen C. Schlesinger, *ACT of Creation—the Founding of the United Nations* (Westview Press, 2003).

Harris O. Schoenberg, *War No More! A Concrete Action Plan to Revitalize the United Nations Security Council* (New York: Center for Public Policy, 1995), 823, United Nations Plaza, New York, NY 10010.

Arkady Shevchenko, *Breaking with Moscow* (Publisher: Knopf, 1985).

Sub regional organizations in Africa:

Economic Community of West African States (ECWAS), Economic Community of Central African States (ECCAS), Community of Sahelo-Saharian States (CSSS), Common Market of Southern and Eastern African States (COMESA), Southern African Development Community (SADEC), East African Community (EAC).

Intergovernmental Authority for Development (IGAD), Union of Arab Maghreb (UMA).

Economic and Monetary Community of Central African States (EMUAS). Community of the Indian Ocean (CIO), Economic and Monetary Union of West African States (EMUWAS).

United Nations General Assembly, A/32/424, December 16, 1977. Letter from the permanent representative of Panama to the United Nations, addressed to the secretary-general, December 2, 1977, regarding the results of the Panama Canal Treaty Referendum.

U Thant, *View from the UN, The Memoirs of U Thant*, Doubleday & Co., Garden City, New York, 1978.

About the Author

Abdelkader Abbadi is a long-time participant in international affairs, working for the thirty years as a staff member at the United Nations Secretariat, and as a journalist for many publications, including the Paris based *Jeune Afrique*. At five, he and the other fun-loving boys of his village were told by the French authorities that they must attend school. With an illiterate mother and a father who could barely read but not write, young Kader found school to be a strange activity. His parents supported him fully, and this was the beginning of his education, which culminated twenty-five years later with a Ph.D. in political science from the University of California at Berkeley.

The recipient of a Fulbright Fellowship in 1958, Abbadi is a shining example of the program's mandate to foster international peace and cooperation through education. At the International House at Berkeley and at the headquarters of the United Nations in New York, Abbadi has worked with others from many other countries, always with the goal of world peace. Married to a woman of Dutch descent, Abbadi today speaks several languages at home to his three children and eight grandchildren.

At work, as a journalist, international staff and diplomat, he is fluent in French, Arabic, Spanish and English. He has learned how to greet the Secretary General Ban Ki-moon in his native Korean.

Today, Abbadi divides his time between New York City, where he reports on North African affairs and international matters, and Hillsdale, New York where he and his wife raise apples, pears, peaches, kiwis, figs and quinces in a backyard orchard in the Berkshire Mountains. That reminds him of the Atlas range at home in Morocco.

www.ingramcontent.com/pod-product-compliance
Lightning Source LLC
Chambersburg PA
CBHW071341280526
45787CB00001B/170